THE SPECIAL YEARS

The Special Years

An Essential Guide for Parents of Under Fives

Celia Bowring

Hodder & Stoughton

LONDON SYDNEY AUCKLAND

British Library Cataloguing in Publication Data
A record for this book is available from the British Library

ISBN 0 340 68672 3

Printed and bound in Great Britain by
Cox & Wyman Ltd, Reading, Berks.

Hodder and Stoughton Ltd
A Division of Hodder Headline PLC
338 Euston Road
London NW1 3BH

This book is dedicated to
Ted and Nena Bartholomew, my parents.
Although they died before our children were born,
their wisdom and love lives on.

ACKNOWLEDGMENTS

I am grateful to the following people for their time, wisdom and encouragement:
Alison Atkinson, Julia Bell, Tamara Bennett, Jonathan Booth, Sheryl Chudley, Serena Colchester, Vivien Corsie, Marian Dmochowska, Guy Hordern, Jane Hastings, Carol Hylton, Nicky Isard, Lindsay Melluish, Judy O'Brien, Rob Parsons, Sheila Ridsdale and Monica Sutton.

I am indebted to Daniel, Emma and Andrew who contributed much to this book and were very patient while I wrote it.

Finally, my deep gratitude to Lyndon who has shared in the partnership of parenting with all his heart and shown me from a father's perspective what it's all about.

CONTENTS

Contents

FOREWORD

I have great sympathy with the man who said, 'The problem with parenting is that just about the time you get experience – you're redundant!' The truth is that the task of raising children is an awesome one, containing the potential for incredible joy and not a little heartache. It would be hard to think of a situation in which we have such responsibility for the life of another person and by definition no experience at it.

I know from our work in CARE for the Family that parents all across the land are asking for support and resources that will help them in the role they have to play. I believe that Celia Bowring has written a book that will become a standard text, read not only by parents of young children but also by those considering parenthood. I cannot stress that last point enough; what we need in the job of parenting is a head-start!

This is above all a practical book: it will help with teething, tantrums and the million and one issues that hit those who care for the very young. It is not just a 'how-to' book however. It is a resource that will help parents mould the lives of their children and give them a strong foundation for life itself.

Whatever the age of our children it is never too late to influence their lives for good, but there is no doubt that when they are very young the opportunities are greater. These are the special years, and once this door of childhood has closed no power on earth can open it again.

I recommend this book with all my heart. It will help you be a better parent and one day you will pass it on, dog-eared and worn, to the child it helped you raise.

Rob Parsons
CARE for the Family

PART ONE
BABIES

1
NEW BEGINNINGS

Mankind owes to the child the best it has to give.
United Nations Declaration

There is nothing quite like finding out you are pregnant! Can any other news have such an impact on your mind and heart as the realisation that, as from now, there is, living inside you, a completely new and unique person who did not exist before? For some it's an unwelcome shock, for others a longed-for dream finally come true, and most of us experience a reaction somewhere in between!

We stared at the test-tube in its plastic holder. Willing the circle in the bottom of it to change colour, we held our breath hardly daring to hope. Lyndon and I were longing to have a baby. We had been married for almost eight years, faced the bitter disappointment of childlessness and now ... it looked like ...

During the next seven years we celebrated two more positive pregnancy tests and have the children to prove it.

CHANGES THAT PREGNANCY BRINGS

Parenthood begins in pregnancy. Although age is counted from the day of our birth, life starts well before that. So that's where we'll start too.

From the day you discover you're pregnant many things are going to be different. Soon you will feel the effects of early pregnancy: tiredness, sickness perhaps, and maybe a change in your tastes for food and drink. If you are fortunate enough

3

to sail through it all with scarcely a twinge, spare a thought for those of us who find the nine months long and tiring as well as a time of excitement and anticipation.

You and your partner, if you have one, will need the period of pregnancy to adjust in readiness for the new arrival who will change your lives! It is just as well that it takes nine months and not nine weeks because you will need more time than you realise, especially if this is your first child.

THE SECRET LIFE WITHIN

During the pregnancy you may spend hours imagining what this new little individual is going to be like. From early on there is a relationship there, between the tiny pre-born child and yourselves. That bond grows stronger as time goes on and the baby makes her presence more and more felt.

Even in the womb the baby can be affected by things going on around her. If the mother smokes, or if she contracts certain illnesses, the child will be affected. By avoiding alcohol and eating properly she can benefit her baby before birth. As well as these medical factors, unborn babies are responsive to many other things in their environment. They can feel, hear and even taste. They become accustomed to the environment of the womb, the gurgles and rhythms inside their mothers' bodies as well as external voices and sounds.

The Secret Life of the Unborn Child, by Thomas Verny with John Kelly, presents the findings of researchers who have studied unborn babies.

By his fifth week, for example, studies show that he is already developing an amazingly complex repertoire of reflex actions. By his eighth week, he is not only moving his head, arms and trunk easily, he has already fash- ioned these movements into a primitive body language – expressing his likes and dislikes with well-placed jerks and kicks. What he especially does not like is being poked at. Push, poke or pinch a mother's stomach and her two-and-a-half-month-old foetus will quickly squirm away (as observed through various techniques).

Facial expressions take a little longer than general body movements to master. By his fourth month, the unborn child can frown, squint and grimace ... Stroke his lips and he starts sucking.

Four to eight weeks later, he is as sensitive to touch as any one-year-old. If his scalp is accidentally tickled during a medical examination, he quickly moves his head. He also vehemently dislikes cold water. If it is injected into his mother's stomach, he kicks violently.

Perhaps the most surprising thing about this thoroughly surprising creature is his discriminating tastes. We do not usually think of the foetus as a gourmet. But he is one – of sorts. Add saccharin to his normally bland diet of amniotic fluid and his swallowing rate doubles. Add a foul-tasting iodine-like oil called Lipidol and those rates not only drop sharply, but he also grimaces.

Recent studies also show that from the twenty-fourth week on, the unborn child listens all the time. And he has a lot to listen to. The pregnant abdomen and uterus are very noisy places. His mother's stomach rumblings are the loudest sounds he hears. Her voice, his father's voice, and other occasional noises are quieter but still audible to him. The sound that dominates his world, though, is the rhythmic thump of the maternal heartbeat. As long as it is at its regular rhythm, the unborn knows all is well; he feels secure and that sense of security stays with him.

Pre-born babies are also susceptible to what we could call their emotional environment. A mother who feels positive, optimistic and emotionally at peace is likely to convey all this through her own body and so to her unborn baby. Of course, every one of us goes through difficult times; it is normal for a pregnant woman to become upset from time to time and she need not worry that this is going to have a bad effect on her baby. But every child flourishes best if he or she is securely accepted, nurtured and loved from the very beginning of life.

Dr Verny describes cases where extreme experiences before birth have led to problems with coming to terms with life and relationships during childhood and on into adult years.

> Obviously his emotional and intellectual needs are far more primitive than ours. The important point is that he has them. He has to feel loved and wanted just as urgently – perhaps even more urgently – than we do. He has to be talked to and thought of; otherwise his spirit and often his body too, begin wilting.
>
> A secure person is deeply self-confident. How can he not be when he has been told from the very edge of consciousness onward that he is wanted and loved?

Both mother and father can give this precious gift to their hidden child. She can talk to him, hold and stroke him within her and take care of herself too. Fathers may feel further removed but can contribute tremendously by making sure the mother feels secure and beloved and they too can communicate directly to their unborn child. Dr Verny continues:

> Virtually everyone who has studied the expectant father's role has found that his support is absolutely essential to [the mother] and thus to their child's well-being ... An equally vital factor is his commitment to the marriage ... A child hears his father's voice *in utero*, and there is solid evidence that hearing that voice makes a big emotional difference. In cases where a man talked to his child *in utero* using short soothing words, the newborn was able to pick out his father's voice in a room even in the first hour or two of life ... he responds to it emotionally. If he's crying, for instance, he'll stop.

It is important to remember that babies are affected by the environment and the way the mother leads her life, but not to be too anxious about the times of emotional upset, sickness or other pressures which we all inevitably experience. Unborn children are remarkably resilient and occasional stress is unlikely to have any bad effects on your baby's physical or emotional health. In fact the occasional upset will positively prepare the baby for the chronically imperfect world into which he is about to be born! The greatest birth-day gift you can give your child is your love, and the security that comes with it. Nobody is perfect, especially not parents, and even though we try our hardest to provide the best possible environment for this new young life, there will always be accidents, mistakes and problems.

We need a balanced and realistic expectation of how things will turn out and must not fall into the trap of wanting everything to be perfect – because it never ever is!

THE GIFT OF BIRTH

There is nothing more precious than the gift of life! Life makes itself known in the wonders of the flying fish and corals of the South Pacific, the beauty of a woodland in the spring, through the sounds of an orchestra, or trees in the wind. For many of us, the most extraordinary experience of life is at the birth of our own baby and the months before it. Suddenly, as if from nowhere, he or she is there, growing, hidden, silent, vulnerable and yet pulsating with potential and power.

Today we can benefit from the amazing advances in technology and scientific knowledge. Previously infertile couples can now often be helped to have a child of their own. With the help of the ultra-sound scan, we can observe unborn children in detail and foresee likely problems and if necessary operate on babies when they are still in the womb!

PREPARED FOR PARENTHOOD

Pregnancy – especially when you are having your first baby – can be a really exciting period of your life. There's so much to discover about what is happening, both to you and your child, as the weeks pass. Sometimes tiredness, discomfort and worry may weigh you down and the pregnancy seems to go on for ever. This season of waiting is very necessary to get ready for the inevitable upheavals your baby will bring to your life! Not just for the woman, either – expectant fathers need to prepare, too.

There are many decisions to be made during pregnancy. Where will the baby be born? What practical preparations should be made? When should I finish work? Will I return to work afterwards, and if so when? Along the way other dilemmas may arise that you were not expecting and these nine months are extremely important and potentially stressful.

Faced with such decisions it is worth keeping two points in mind. First, that there are many sources of information and counsel – books, magazines, seminars, courses as well as the people who are there to help you. But the second principle is that, having read, listened, discussed and observed all you can, you should feel confident, as future parents, to do as you think best, whatever your friends and relations say – and they undoubtedly will!

Begin to think about the practical, financial and emotional changes the baby will bring – especially the different way you will feel about your partner – from early on. A woman can feel isolated from her partner during pregnancy, especially if she thinks he is uninterested in her state. In one sense, *you are both* pregnant and the more you can talk about it the better!

A WORD FOR FATHERS

While she is expecting the baby, and for some months afterwards, your partner will undergo major upheavals and changes in her body. Certain hormones needed to sustain the pregnancy will have side effects on her, ranging from sickness to aching muscles and feeling emotionally fragile at times. As her normal figure vanishes she finds she is less agile. Fears for the baby's health, apprehension about the birth itself, uncertainty that she will really cope with motherhood are among the hundreds of matters pre-occupying her. She may not always be rational about all this – don't panic if you fail to understand her swings of mood, strange fixations or lack of self-worth and confidence. Your love and support will make all the difference and you will both enjoy the days when she is on top of the world!

There are plenty of opportunities to express tender loving care. Make the most of the last opportunities to go out without paying for babysitters or worrying to be back in time for the next feed! Plan some treats – a meal out, a trip to the cinema or whatever else is your favourite thing to do. But don't be surprised if she is feeling permanently tired, and make sure she rests enough. If you don't wish your romantic evening to be marred by her nodding off during the opening credits of the film or yawning over her Big Mac, insist on a proper rest in bed that afternoon.

The summer Yvonne was half-way through having her first baby, her husband, Brian, planned a surprise for her. 'Be ready,' he said, 'at two o'clock, because I'm taking you somewhere really special.' Her mind worked overtime. Somewhere really nice for tea perhaps? A visit to the theatre? Yvonne dressed in her best, even discarding her unsightly but comfortable shoes in favour of a pair with heels. The surprise turned out to be a tour to the Chelsea Flower Show, which was so busy that day that the couple could not find a place to sit or a refreshment stand without a queue fifty people deep! She didn't have the heart to tell him how drained and exhausted she felt that day. 'My feet were on fire and I thought my lower half would come away from the rest of me. So we admired the roses and the bonsai trees, the hydrangeas and the pelargoniums until mercifully we got back in the car and came home!' That surprise didn't work out too well (although they've laughed about it since) but there were many others which were great fun and took their minds off the bump and drew them closer as the date approached. Hours spent sharing and communicating are vital at every stage in marriage, not least when you are expecting a baby.

In Leonie's fourth pregnancy the muscles in her insteps were overstretched and very painful at the end of the day. She was so grateful for her husband gently massaging her poor feet one evening that, overcome with life in general and being pregnant in particular, Leonie burst into tears! His understanding and love were so important to her, cheered her up, and soon they were laughing over this bizarre way of spending an evening off!

Not many men feel the compulsion to read up about the process of pregnancy and few women would particularly want to discuss the finer points of obstetrics over breakfast. But at some juncture, a bit of information will be useful; and if you plan to be there on the day you'll definitely need to know something about labour and how a baby is born. Antenatal classes which are run for pregnant women to teach them what to do when they are giving birth always include a session or two for men too. The National Childbirth Trust offers antenatal preparation for couples, tailored to their needs; for example, an eight-week course of two-hour sessions, held in the evening. Please make an effort to go: you certainly won't be the only male there feeling like a trespasser on feminine territory. Look on it as a training exercise or seminar about a job you will be involved in within the next few months.

MAKING LOVE IN PREGNANCY

And then there's your sexual relationship. If you are both content to continue love-making right through the pregnancy, well and good. (Apart from a few adjustments as your wife's abdomen changes in size and shape.) But be ready to recognise that she may feel differently about it. Some women lose much of their libido, especially near the end. Others may fear the baby could be harmed. (Ask the doctor for reassurance on this.) Many are so tired they feel lovemaking is just one more physical demand on their bodies.

Women's libido, however, can dramatically increase during the middle three months of pregnancy. This is absolutely nothing to worry about!

It is vital to talk about how you both feel. Undercurrents of rejection, frustration, isolation and misunderstanding can mount up and cause a rift between you. Give and take on both sides is needed ... and a good sense of humour.

HOME ALONE

Perhaps you are on your own and there isn't an involved father for your baby. This is going to be a time for your mother, sister or a close reliable girl friend to come alongside and give you the support you need. Don't feel you have to go through it alone. Think about who you could ask and go ahead and approach her sooner rather than later.

Mary Anne, from South Africa, became pregnant while staying in the UK. Her first reaction was to have an abortion, but her Christian faith – put aside for some years – became important to her again and as she began to ask God what to do in her impossible predicament she decided she could not destroy the life within her. Fortunately her new friends at church really supported her and promised to give her any help she might need. Mary Anne considered adoption but in the end decided to keep her baby. In the last weeks of pregnancy she moved in with a friend who drove her to hospital and stayed with her for eighteen hours of labour. 'I couldn't have gone through it alone,' she said. 'And I didn't have a clue about feeding or anything, but Christine showed me so much and eventually I got used to it all!'

Parenthood is one of the greatest challenges in life. We all need as much support as we can get.

2

PARENTS IN WAITING

Before I got married I had six theories about bringing
up children; now I have six children and no theories.
John Wilmot, Earl of Rochester, 1647-80

Expectant mothers need to take the responsibility of taking
proper care of themselves – and as a result, the growing
unborn baby.

ANTENATAL CARE

When you discover you are having a baby your first port of
call will be your GP, who can confirm you are pregnant and
discuss plans with you. Shortly after this will come a rather
lengthy visit to the hospital antenatal clinic, where you will
be asked umpteen questions, undergo various examinations
and perhaps some tests. As the pregnancy progresses there
will be regular check-ups, further tests and ultra-sound
examinations.

Never be frightened to ask if you don't understand what
is being done. Most of your antenatal treatment will be
monitoring your health and the progress of the baby;
checking that there are no problems affecting the pregnancy. Some tests are to detect possible abnormalities in
your baby and you may wish to think very carefully about
the implications of undergoing such investigations. There
are risks involved, the results are not unfailingly accurate
and if some tests are positive you will be offered an
abortion. For instance, an amnio-centesis could indicate

spina-bifida or Down's syndrome. Make sure you have all the information you need, and take time to talk through these issues.

Happily almost every pregnancy will be untroubled by complications and antenatal appointments become part of a reassuring routine. One of the most exciting moments of pregnancy is the first view of your baby on an ultra-sound scan screen – your first baby video! This appointment is a must for expectant fathers if at all possible. Lyndon was so excited to see our first baby on TV, the staff nearly had to ask him to leave!

PRACTICAL PREPARATIONS

Although being pregnant seems to last for ever, it is just as well to have a long time to get ready for the baby.

There are practical arrangements to be made. It is very tempting to be persuaded by glossy catalogues, attractive displays in shops and the pressure of others around when it comes to buying for the baby. What do babies actually need, and how much should be obtained before the birth?

Of course it is natural to want to shop around, buying that irresistible sleep-suit and choosing pretty furnishings for the baby's bedroom. Be honest, these purchases are for you, not the infant, who will be oblivious to her surroundings for many weeks yet. Don't rule out the use of second-hand clothes and equipment. You will discover other parents who are happy to pass around their first-size outfits, and you can spend the money you saved on a meal out together – much more beneficial to your child!

It is not easy to gauge what is best to buy. Everyone is slightly different in what they feel is essential but the following list may be a useful starting point.

WHAT YOU WILL NEED

Large equipment

Carry-cot and wheels. This can serve a variety of purposes; as a pram, a travel cot and as a place to sleep in the house. I found having a second carry-cot useful so that I didn't have to take it up and down stairs all the time.

Cot. When your baby grows too big for a carry-cot he will need to sleep in a cot for the next few years. This needs to be sturdy, and if it is second-hand make sure the mattress is in good condition and in line with safety regulations. Use lead-free paint when repainting any baby equipment.

Pushchair. This too will need to stand up to a lot of wear and tear. Pushchairs usually last for about one and a half children! If you are putting a young baby in it (about six weeks onwards), do make sure it is properly designed, with adequate back support and a lie-back mechanism.

Car seat. By law all children must be safely restrained in cars. It is esssential *always* to use a car seat that is designed for the age of your baby – right from birth. If buying a second-hand one, be certain that it has not been involved in an accident, making it unsafe. Car seats are actually very useful as they can double up as a seat in the house and allow you to lift a sleeping baby from the car without disturbing her.

High chair. From about eight months, well bolstered with cushions, this will be a useful piece of equipment not just for mealtimes but for the baby to sit in and play nearby, while you get on with other things. There are many variations of high chairs but do make quite sure yours is safe, as falls from this height can be very nasty. *Always strap small children in!*

Baby bouncer. This is great for young babies (eight weeks onwards) whose back muscles do not yet give enough support for an ordinary seat. It gives them the grandstand view of life they enjoy and the pleasant feeling of rocking as they bounce gently in it. *Always use this on the floor.* It will slide as the baby bounces and could edge over a bed or work top. Second-hand ones are usually easy to come by and are fairly cheap.

Baby sling. All babies love to be held and carried! A sling allows you to do this and something else at the same time. Many people put their tiny babies in slings when out for a walk so they can enjoy the close warmth of human contact rather than just being pushed in a pram. I have found a sling invaluable around the house when there are many things to do and the baby is fretful. Fathers often enjoy carrying a baby like this too.

Clothes. There are some beautiful designs available for babies and it is fun to dress your son or daughter in attractive clothes. It is, though, worth remembering that they will grow out of the first few sizes very quickly, so many of your 'newborn' garments can be borrowed or bought second-hand. As well as a good supply of vests, Babygros and woollens, you'll need warm outdoor clothes and a selection of shawls and blankets.

Nappies. You'll need to decide whether to go for the traditional towelling or modern disposable types (although disposables are specially useful for holidays, etc., even if you use ordinary nappies the rest of the time). Buy a dozen muslin squares. They come in handy to mop up all the thrills and spills of babyhood, especially during feeding time!

Bottles. If you are breast-feeding you won't need to get into the routine of sterilising bottles and teats unless you use a bottle for water. Otherwise you will have to get a sterilising unit along with all the other necessary kit for bottle-feeding. It is very important to keep high standards of hygiene and cleanliness in all aspects of baby care. Their resistance to infection is low, especially in the early weeks and months.

Many of our parents or grandparents began life sleeping in a wooden drawer, and had none of the advantages of fold-up, lie-back buggies, electric bottle warmers or throwaway nappies. It must have all been a lot simpler then! – although modern parents can consider themselves most fortunate to be able to use the labour-saving ideas of today.

MOTHERS AND WORK

Next time Mothering Sunday comes around do something special for your mum if she is still with you. Women who stay at home with their pre-school children work just as hard, if not harder, than anyone else. They receive no wage, are at the mercy of others' needs and schedules and are often taken for granted. Day after day, carrying out the complex, repetitive, demanding and never-ending jobs involved in raising a family and caring for the home deserves all the appreciation and encouragement there is going! If you are 'just a housewife', take stock of all the things you actually do, the skills and expertise you have acquired and the achievements you clock up each week and year. Although much of what we do is mundane and unexciting, the long-term effects of being a home-working mother are manifold and greatly benefit families and society as a whole.

However the old assumption that all mothers will stay at home to provide full-time care for their children is no longer automatic. In 1981, 25 per cent of mothers with a child under five years were working full- or part-time, but by 1991 this had risen to 47 per cent, fuelling demands for child care (LandMARC).

Some mothers need to work to keep the family going, especially lone parents. Mothers employed outside the home still have to fit in all the domestic chores. Even in the Nineties, husbands are not always eager to do their fair share of the washing, shopping, cleaning, ironing and childcare – but many, of course, are absolutely wonderful!

Others do not wish to break off their professional careers and there are women who feel that twenty-four-hours-a-day undiluted motherhood would drive them crazy and do not believe they should surrender the freedom and stimulation their job brings and stay at home. Do not underestimate your own needs as a person. Once your child is old enough, is there some way you can work from home or share child care with a friend, so that each of you is free for a few sessions?

Debbie has two children, one aged a year, the other three. When each was born she took the allowed maternity leave from her job as an anaesthetist and then returned on a part-time basis. She left her sons with a registered child minder when she went to work.

Whatever you decide, make sure you fill in the necessary forms early in pregnancy to receive your statutory rights and leave your options as open as possible. You may not know what will work best until the baby is born. You have a range of options:

mother at home with child;
child in own home with close relative;
child in close relative's home;
child in own home with qualified carer;
child in another home with qualified carer;
child in institutionalised care.

Naturally any person you employ must be qualified and/or registered by your local authority, with good references. You may be fortunate enough to have a family member who will be able and willing to give you support. You must also decide how you will manage when your child is unwell.

As time passes the decisions you make before the birth may be adapted; the shape of your life, the demands of the baby and your own needs will alter year by year. Keep reviewing the situation.

3

THE GRAND ARRIVAL

Help me to remember, Lord, that nothing's gonna
happen today that you and me can't handle together.
Traditional

The worst scenario for most pregnant women would be to
go into labour on a busy day in the middle of a supermarket, trolley overflowing with frozen peas and Bran
Flakes. Can you imagine the embarrassment and inconve-
nience? This actually happened to Annie, but being a born
exhibitionist she enjoyed every moment of the fuss she
caused! The mainly middle-aged female staff were wonderfully calm and sensible, she was put into an ambulance and
her abandoned shopping returned to the shelves.

GOING INTO LABOUR

To quote that famous advertisement, 'Any time, any
place, anywhere ...' the onset of labour is unpredict-
able. Towards the end of pregnancy the uterine muscles
seem to go into serious training and often these contractions are so strong they seem like the real thing. I
remember spending anxious hours in the middle of the
night, timing my pains with a stop watch as I searched in
the pregnancy book to compare what they said labour
really was like with how I felt. It can be difficult to know
when or if to phone the hospital. Every birth is individual
and as unborn babies don't read the manuals, events
often turn out differently from how you might have

expected! It is not uncommon to arrive at the maternity wing only to be sent home again feeling very sheepish because the child is not yet ready to be born and the contractions have ceased.

You may choose to have your baby at home and this practice is becoming more common. Ask your GP about the possibility. Unless there are real concerns about complications during your labour or other factors there is no reason why you should not enjoy the comforts and familiarity of home when you have your baby. You will be assigned to a midwife who will give all the help and care you need, before, during and after the birth. Although this option is becoming more popular again, the vast majority of women have their children in the local maternity hospital. There are other options too – ask your GP. If there is a choice of maternity hospitals, take time to visit each one before you decide. They often differ a great deal.

With a first baby, the labour is often slow and long so there is probably no huge urgency to get to hospital as soon as things start. Only if your waters break – hopefully not in public! – or when strong, regular, painful contractions are coming every seven or eight minutes or so is it time to go. First have something to eat and drink, and check you have all you need because it may be a while before you see home again.

Some women are already in-patients as there have been difficulties during the pregnancy. Trisha had this experience with her baby. Because he was not growing as he should, she was ordered to bed and lived in the hospital on and off for two months prior to the birth. Unfortunately this stay coincided with a strike of hospital workers, which meant that all the food was cooked elsewhere and served on paper plates, the ward was inadequately cleaned and the sheets were made of disposable paper! Trisha was glad when they let her out at weekends! Finally the doctors decided to induce the birth by piercing the amniotic sac to break the waters and start the labour. So Jack arrived exactly on the day he was due – unlike her other boys, one of whom came five days late and the other three weeks early!

For months you may have been ticking off each day, but do plan on being kept waiting, then the disappointment if that red letter day comes and goes will not be so acute.

USEFUL THINGS TO PACK FOR HOSPITAL

*Spare nightdresses with front openings suitable for breast-feeding if you plan to.

*Nursing bras, panties (paper ones are good) and Dr White's maternity pads. If you are breast-feeding, breast pads and, if advised, ointment for sore nipples – ask your pharmacist.

*Washing kit, mirror, make-up and perfume.

*Shawl, lightweight dressing gown and slippers.

*Lots of coins for the phone and/or a phone card.

*Address book.

*Writing paper, birth announcement cards.

*A picnic. When you've finished having your baby you may be famished and there may be no food available on the ward.

*Baby shawl.

*A couple of sets of clothes for the baby.

*Nappies.

*Muslin squares.

*A riveting book!

*Knitting or sewing.

*A personal stereo and tapes.

ARRIVING AT HOSPITAL

When you arrive, you will be booked in and examined to see how far labour has progressed. Depending on how much the cervix has opened to allow the child through – it needs to stretch ten centimetres wide – the midwife will know how far advanced you are. In the early stages you can walk around, take a bath and generally relax but when the contractions become stronger you may be less free to move about.

At this point there may be particular things you want to happen. Would listening to some favourite music help? Are you really most comfortable lying on your back or would you feel better in a different position – squatting, kneeling or standing? There will be certain restrictions – in some cases a monitor may be fitted through your cervix on to the baby's scalp to monitor his heart rate, you could have a belt round you attached to other recording machinery or you might be plugged into a drip.

WILL IT HURT?

Yes, basically. But today we have great advantages in childbirth. Skill, technology and pain relief are all available – but so too will be inner resources you may never have realised were there. There will have been opportunities earlier in the pregnancy to discuss the various methods of pain relief and make a 'birth plan' to act as a guideline to your preferences. (But this is not guaranteed to work – babies are not notified about such things and may have another agenda!) Some hospitals may allow your child to be born under water or using other more traditional methods. Whatever your choice, to go for an unusual approach or to leave things to the discretion of the staff, the most important thing to remember is that you have a right to express how you feel; *this is your baby, not the hospital's!* and the more you can work together as a team the better.

Now is the time to put into practice all the techniques you learned in the antenatal classes. The best thing to be said for contractions is that they come and go. With or without pain relievers you can weather each wave, recognising the rhythm of the tightening and relaxing of each one. Now and again you may be tempted to panic, but please be brave, it's worth it all in the end. I have never felt so helpless and vulnerable as on that birthing bed, and the loving encouragement of Lyndon and those around me meant so much.

Even if you find the hospital environment intimidating, as far as possible you should feel in control of your situation. Our GP gave us some good advice; that the father – or whoever else is with you – should act as a go-between between the woman and the professionals in the room. You will communicate your needs, concerns and questions more easily to the person you know well and he or she can make sure they are met. Taking on this very important role helps a father feel part of what is happening.

When the baby's head begins to emerge, the mother's vagina is stretched – as you can imagine! The muscles of the uterus push so hard that it can actually cause a tear. It is worth discussing this with the doctor and midwife well ahead of time, and decide, if this does happen to you, whether or not to have an episiotomy, which is a cut made to avoid this tear – which many say will heal less easily. The after-effects of either can be painful, so do make sure you receive the best treatment for you and minimise any problems. Many mothers need some stitches once the baby is born. An injection will anaesthetise the area and you may not even notice the doctor busily repairing any lesion while you feast your eyes on the baby. You will feel sore afterwards, but normally it will quickly heal and the stitches dissolve within a week or ten days.

THE DELIVERY

The moment of birth, common to every human being, is nothing short of a miracle. This person, who has been hidden, tied up to nature's life-support system within her mother's body for the best part of a year, now makes her individual journey into the world. The arrival of a child is a solemn yet stunning event and those first minutes should be special.

Once the baby is out and the umbilical cord cut, the staff will check her breathing and other life functions, clean her up and hand her, probably crying now, back to you. Now you can ask to be left alone, just the three of you to be together. As soon as possible take your baby close to you and try to nurse her at your breast; stroking her and talking to her softly. This is a very important time for her dad too, to have close contact and begin to get to know his new child. Although the focus of parenthood has been on the mother for the last nine months, she is just as much her father's daughter!

SPECIAL CARE

Unfortunately this cosy getting-to-know-you session may be impossible. Sometimes the medics need to take over, there may be problems and certainly in the case of premature babies you will have to cope with life in the special care baby unit for a while.

Ginny was rushed to hospital in late November. She was in labour but only twenty weeks into her pregnancy. She and Jon waited anxiously over the next hours as the contractions responded to medication and ceased. Day followed day and turned to weeks. Christmas came and went and finally they reached the crucial twenty-six-week point. Shortly afterwards Donald was born weighing in at a mere 850 grams. 'Then we had months of him in the Special Care Unit. Being so premature, he had all kinds of problems – was on a ventilator, wired to a monitor inside his centrally-heated incubator and was drip-fed through tubes. We spent as much time with him as we could, gently stroking him where he lay, so tiny and fragile, and willed him to live. In February we triumphantly brought him home!'

Donald is now nearly two and doing famously.

We can never know what life holds in store for us. Patricia's pregnancy had gone two weeks past the due date and there was talk of inducing her. Unfortunately, the obstetrician did not realise the baby was in the breech position (coming feet first) and Richard ended up being born by an emergency Caesarian. He had one 'clicky' hip and the other dislocated. Far more serious was the consultant's news. He explained to Patricia and Andy that their baby had cystic fibrosis. In a state of exhaustion and shock they wondered fearfully what the future would hold.

We all hope fervently for a healthy baby, but sometimes families have to face the reality of a child's illness or disability. There is little anyone can say to ease the pain you will feel, but always keep your hopes alive – the initial diagnosis may turn out to have been exaggerated and probably much can be done. As parents, you can give your love to your baby, accepting him just as he is while you co-operate with the doctors and nurses who are working so hard to improve his condition.

EARLY DAYS

Your newborn will be no stranger to you; because his life began months before, he will feel familiar to you when you finally meet face to face.

After a well-earned cup of tea you will be washed and gently dressed in fresh clothes. Meanwhile your partner can start making the necessary phone calls to spread the news abroad.

Once settled in the postnatal ward with all the other new mothers there will be time to examine your baby at more leisure. He will spend most of his time asleep, waking every few hours to be fed and made comfortable, and by now you will have decided whether to feed your baby yourself or by bottle. Breast-feeding, even for the first few days, gives a great start in life because human milk is made to exactly the right formula. A mother's supply of milk is stimulated and established by the baby's sucking, but before your proper milk 'comes in', on or about the fourth day, the baby takes in wonderful stuff called colostrum which is basically the water, sugar, protein and minerals for energy and nutrition. Colostrum also transfers important antibodies present in your body to the baby, which will protect him from infection until he builds up his own immune system. Breast milk also does this, later.

If, however, it will be necessary to leave your child while he is still very young or you have other reasons for being unable to breast-feed, rest assured that the manufactured formula milk is excellent; many strapping adults are walking around today fit and healthy on the strength of it.

Breast-feeding may seem a difficult skill to master, but do persevere, it is not only the best for your baby but more convenient for you too. In the hospital there will be people to help and advise you, and most women soon find their own way to hold the baby in a relaxed way to make the experience a positive one. You may find your nipples becoming sore, and an uncomfortable fullness when a feed is due, but do soldier on if you can! It should get easier. The National Childbirth Trust has experienced counsellors who will help you, free of charge. Find the group in your area and make the most of the friendly and practical advice and support they can offer.

Caring for a very young baby is a surprisingly exhausting and all-consuming occupation; don't be surprised that you have no time for anything else. Make your own well-being a priority in these early days; if you do not eat well and get sufficient rest you will find it dificult to get over the birth and the demands of caring for the infant. Do not underestimate the support needed to sustain this new lifestyle successfully – and so long as you do not expect to sleep for more than two hours at any one time you'll be fine!

While you are in hospital, take advantage of every opportunity to rest. If this is your first baby, make the most of the specially trained nurses who will gladly teach you the ropes of caring for a baby. When our first was born, although I had done my best to read up on the subject and had occasionally looked after my friends' babies for a few hours, I really was pretty clueless. There seemed so much to learn and I was apprehensive that this funny, scrawny, pimply creature was my own responsibility. In a few days I would leave the security of the postnatal ward and look after him all on my own. Lyndon knew even less about babies than me – it would be a total miracle if the child survived!

COPING WITH THE 'BLUES'

Two-thirds of all mothers are affected by the 'baby blues' in the first ten days after birth – often on the third or fourth day when the breast milk 'comes in'. This is not usually serious; the total upheaval brought about by birth will affect most women emotionally.

At the time our third child was born, there was the distressing case of a baby snatched from a London hospital by a woman posing as a health visitor. This situation haunted me – far more than the usual sympathy and concern I would normally feel – and I remember that on the day the news came through that the child had been found and safely restored to her mother, I wept copiously and felt almost as if it was my own baby that had been stolen and found.

The more we are aware of our possible emotional fragility and can share how we feel with those close to us, the better. Often it is the woman's partner who notices the beginnings of depression and can play an important part in getting help for her. A serious case of postnatal depression may then be avoided. If you are feeling dreadful – seek help, from your doctor or another appropriate professional.

Laurie was usually very outgoing, but after her second daughter was born she lost all interest in life. She felt numb and distant from all the excitement going on around her. Laurie managed to cover up how she felt and ploughed on day by day with the demands of life. 'I was in a dark tunnel, felt a failure and wanted to go to sleep and never wake up,' she remembers.

Postnatal depression can come on for many reasons and can be relieved with professional help. If you think you are suffering from it, don't just soldier on – go to see your doctor at once! Otherwise you risk a condition which could continue for months or even years.

ADJUSTING TO FATHERHOOD

This will be a time of considerable adjustment for the new father too. He needs to come to terms with a lot of changes.

1. He will have to accept a decrease in the sexual relationship for a while. It will have been difficult during the pregnacy to continue the same level of sexual activity as before. Because she will be extremely tender and will bleed for some time, intercourse will be inappropriate for quite a while.

2. He will need to be sensitive towards the emotions of his partner. With the arrival of the new baby there has come into her life a whole new set of responsibilities, fears, feelings and frustrations. It will take a while for it to fall into place so that she is able to respond to him in a close adult relationship. Be understanding, interested and patient with her!

3. Few young men have a realistic notion of what life with a newborn is like. A new father will have to adjust to the fact that for the time being the household will revolve entirely around this small but vocal individual. His partner will probably seem a bit obsessed with feeds, bringing up wind, baby clothes, nappies and all the other paraphernalia of baby care. He can help by being involved whenever possible and reassuring her she is doing a fantastic job.

4. As the reality of fatherhood begins to dawn, a new dad may feel unsure of his present and future role. Criticism from his understandably stressed wife about something unimportant like the way he puts on a nappy could discourage him from being involved with the baby. When

mothers are positive everyone benefits, as Dad takes his role seriously, and starts to enjoy it.

The best advice for new dads may come from other men who have passed through that initial 'learning curve' of parenthood. The contribution a father can make to the well-being and development of his children is immeasurable; both sons and daughters need fathers – bringing up the kids is by no means just the woman's job. And before too long there will grow inside you a bond with them you could never have dreamt of.

So, as you gaze into the crinkly, toothless face of your newborn, in the world for only a matter of hours, brace yourselves for many interrupted nights and demanding days. But be warned! The time will pass quickly, you will soon be freezing on the sidelines watching his first football match. Make the most of parenthood, right from the beginning.

4
COMING HOME

Any one who says 'I slept like a baby,' obviously has never lived with one. An experienced parent is one who has learned how to fall asleep while the baby wasn't looking.

From time to time a baby is born to someone really 'important'. The world's cameras line up on the pavement. Limousines sweep up and journalists make notes while a breeze of expectation and excitement ripples round the assembled crowd. At last the doors open, a bevy of nurses and aides come out bearing flowers, bags and fluffy blankets and then follow the celebrities themselves, carrying their baby. The people cheer, the flashbulbs flash and viewers see it all on the evening news.

It was different for us, bringing our first baby home from hospital! We left in a flurry of total public disinterest and anonymity and had to stop on the way home for Lyndon to dash into the chemist's for a rubber cushion for my poor stitched-up undercarriage to sit on! In considerable pain, the car parked on double yellow lines with hazard lights flashing, I had to pacify my mewling infant, persuade a traffic warden not to book us and curb my impatience all at once!

A NEW CHAPTER

Still, even if ordinary people don't attract the same attention as the rich and famous, their baby's journey from hospital to home is just as important. Once there, the child is fully the parents' responsibility and a new chapter of life begins. Fortunately new parents are not left to their own devices; hopefully plenty of family and friends will come under the load and help. Do not underestimate the emotional experience of coming home with a new baby – it is a special occasion that often sticks in the memory for a long time.

Richard and Tessa lived in a small house on the outskirts of Reading. They had only been married for a year when Donna was born. Richard said:

I'll never forget the day Tessa and I brought her home. We were like a pair of kids! We had to show this baby every room in the house, introduce her to the cat, let her see all the things we'd got for her room. I remember then how wonderful it felt, sitting on the sofa watching Tess feed her – my own daughter! Soon everyone started arriving and it was busy, busy – but that picture will never leave me. Tessa, Donna and me, our own little family, together in our home!

Jenny arrived home still feeling shell-shocked after James's birth. Unfortunately the moment she walked through the door everyone expected her to do everything she usually did. The kitchen was a bit of a mess, there was a huge pile of ironing and the laundry basket was overflowing. The two older children arrived home from school hungry for their tea but all Jenny needed was to sleep, be alone with the baby and not have to deal with all the normal running of a busy household. Her husband did what he could, but he hadn't slept much either and was not really accustomed to being a substitute mum! When Jenny's parents arrived the next day to take care of them all, everyone was very pleased to see them!

It is very special if grandparent/child relationships can begin at the very start of each baby's life. We could never have managed without Lyndon's parents who, at the news of each birth, have journeyed to London from Wales and looked after us so lovingly and efficiently.

CARE AND SUPPORT

Besides family and friends, the professional carers will arrive on each of those first days at home. When the hospital discharges you and your baby, the community midwives are notified and arrange daily visits until the baby is nine days old. The midwife will monitor the mother's recovery, check the baby's progress and be ready with encouragement and advice about feeding and other aspects of baby care. On the tenth day your health visitor will come instead and from then on you will be welcome to see her at the weekly baby clinic to have the baby weighed and checked, and if you have a particular worry, the clinic doctor will be available.

Charlie was born a couple of weeks early but he was a good weight and thriving. His parents brought him home and the family began to settle down with its newest addition. At about four days old the visiting midwife seemed concerned and after a further test phoned to tell Charlie's parents to take him straight back to the hospital. He was suffering from jaundice and turning a deeper shade of yellow by the hour because his liver wasn't functioning properly. Mild cases of jaundice are quite common in newborn babies and as soon as their livers begin to work efficiently the effects disappear on their own. Charlie's case was slightly more serious. He was readmitted to hospital for two days and put under a special fluorescent light. He was very sleepy and reluctant to feed but finally the family could be reunited again and Charlie was none the worse for his adventure.

LOOKING AFTER YOUR BABY

At this early stage of life, babies' requirements are very basic. They must be kept safe, warm and comfortable, be given nourishment at frequent intervals and from the earliest days need the continual loving contact of their principal carer – usually the mother.

Staying warm

It is very important to bring the baby into a warm home after the hothouse atmosphere of hospital. Much of the heat loss will be through the head, so keep that covered. In the winter, make sure he is kept in an even, warm atmosphere, especially at night, when the temperature in the house drops. The room should be maintained at about 68°F (20°C) for the first couple of weeks. If a baby gets too cold, he is in danger of chilling because as a newborn he is not as good at keeping warm as older humans and needs to use all his energy for the task of living and growing. Be careful not to allow your baby to become overheated either as this can be just as unsafe. Dress him in several light layers and a shawl and try to stick to natural materials that 'breathe' rather than synthetics. Cot duvets are not advisable for young babies, flannel sheets and woollen blankets are better.

Keeping clean

Young babies don't get very dirty – barring accidents! – and there is little point in bathing them every day or changing them into different clothes at night. In a few months' time your washing machine and bath tub will work overtime to keep up with the incredible amount of mess generated by a toddler, but for now your baby will stay clean, and a gentle 'top and tail' wash with cotton wool and warm water is adequate from day to day. Use the time you might have spent undressing, bathing, drying, re-dressing and calming the child – who will not have enjoyed any of it! – just cuddling her a little extra. When you do bath her, make sure everything you need is at hand before you begin, that the room is very warm and the water is just right. The best way to check the temperature is by dipping your elbow in. Your hand, used to hot water, is less sensitive. You can buy baby bath temperature indicators if you don't trust your own judgment.

A newborn's skin is very delicate, so keep to plain water for washing and perhaps a little baby oil for dry patches or cradle cap (flaking skin on the scalp). There will probably be spots and pimples on her face for the first few weeks. That need not worry you. Check that the washing powder or conditioner you use on her clothes does not irritate the skin. The process of being born sometimes leaves its own marks but in almost every case these will vanish and your baby may even look as angelic as the ones in the nappy advertisements!

It will not be long before you master that most noble of arts: changing a dirty nappy! It is amazing how quickly you take this task in your stride and become immune to its more unpleasant aspects. I can never believe the way the smelly contents sometimes leak out, up the back, almost into the ears of the most innocuous-looking little baby.

As well as keeping the nappy area clean, check the stump of the umbilical cord. The midwife will have shown you how to use a special sterilised wipe, and so long as there is no discharge or redness it will quickly heal and the last part of that lifeline that bound you both together for so many months will fall off after a few more days. The emotional and practical ties of parenthood last rather longer!

FEEDING

It takes hours each day to feed a baby, and life will be dominated by it for some weeks. If your child is taking formula milk, others can share the job with the mother. If you breast-feed, you are the only person who will do unless you use a pump to express breast milk to be given to the baby when you are not there. Until solid foods are introduced at about three or four months old – your health visitor will give you advice about the best time for your baby – milk is the sole means of nourishment. Mother's milk is the first choice from the baby's point of view, and women who breast-feed find it a deeply satisfying experience, especially once the early days are past and the milk supply is established. There is plenty of excellent advice available, from family and friends, professionals, the National Childbirth Trust, pamphlets and books.

Sometimes practical ideas like altering the way you sit, arranging a few pillows or taking a good drink as you feed can make things easier. Watch carefully that your nipples do not become sore; keep them dry between feeds, using a special pad to soak up any excess milk. Make sure the baby does not 'chew', but that the areola is right inside the mouth before he latches on. You may find a rubber nipple shield helpful, and there are various other ways your health visitor can advise as you care for this very tender part of your body.

Years ago babies were fed by the clock. No amount of hunger screams from the baby or desperation on the part of the mother were permitted to relax the prescribed routine. It is now believed better to 'feed on demand'. Although at times it can seem very inconvenient, sometimes tiring and too frequent, feeding a baby is a wonderfully positive act of love. Equally as important as the physical need of nourishment is the close human contact and emotional security your child gains as he lies in your arms and blissfully sucks. Get into the habit of caressing and speaking softly to him and make the time one when you communicate your love into the recesses of the infant subconscious. Babies vary in how much cuddling they want, and it is helpful to recognise your own child's need and adapt to it.

When he wakes at night, though, be sure to stay almost silent, feed him in the dark and make it as boring as possible! This may help him realise that normal people sleep between ten and six o'clock. If night feeds are fun, he'll look forward to waking for one even after he is old enough to last until morning.

SLEEPING

One of a baby's main occupations is sleeping, even if it doesn't seem that way to parents trying to survive wakeful nights with a miserable infant! They sleep and wake when their bodies tell them to – for a newborn the word 'routine' has absolutely no relevance or meaning!

There is nothing to stop parents from introducing a routine though, at an early stage. The weeks will quickly pass and the newborn stage will be over soon. Recognise the constants in your baby's body clock and try to plan your day round, say, feeds at seven, ten, one, four and seven o'clock during the day and as few as you can during the night!

Sleep-times can become more definite as the child grows older. Going to bed at night needs to have a different feel to it than daytime naps.

Louise found that none of her three babies were very keen to be put down to go off to sleep by themselves, but she persevered. 'From about three months I put them in their beds and left them awake, even if they cried a little. Because I kept popping back to reassure them without getting them up again, they finally learned to go to sleep alone.' These children are now six, four and two years old and slept through the night from early on.

There are plenty of ways to encourage your baby to settle for sleep. The first important factor is your own attitude. Be positive and give the impression that you assume it will happen. Have key words, phrases and a certain tone of voice that cue the child about what is expected.

Carry out the same actions each night, such as taking him to the window to say goodnight to whatever you can see through it, drawing the curtains and pulling back the bed covers. Perhaps you will turn on a night light or start a special music cassette. A kiss, a smile to reassure the child that you will be nearby may help. Even if your baby is too young to interpret all these messages, put them into the routine, and day by day he will begin to understand. Use a scaled down version of this ritual for daytime naps.

Ceri discovered that her baby son was almost always pacified by sucking, even when he wasn't hungry or thirsty. She would scrub her hands, trim the nail of her little finger and Sam would suck busily away to his heart's content. Once he was asleep she'd gingerly draw her finger away and escape.

Two out of Lizzie's three babies were 'sucky' types. One of them at eighteen months still liked a special piece of cloth to sleep with; the other grew out of that at a year old. Whatever you think about pacifiers, using one might help you get through a difficult patch. One of Lizzie's boys had a soother for about six weeks; it made him drop off to sleep like nothing else. Then, quite abruptly, he lost interest, spat it out each time she offered it and dozed off happily without it from then on.

Many people recommend swaddling babies for bed, tucking a soft, slightly stretchy shawl round over the shoulder and behind the back to make a chrysalis-like bundle snugly wrapped and ready to sleep.

Always make sure that breathing is unrestricted. It is recommended now that babies should be put 'back to bed', as sleeping on their stomachs is thought to be more associated with cot deaths. Sudden infant death syndrome ('cot death') is obviously devastating for a family. Every parent tiptoes into their baby's room to check him as he sleeps and there is nothing worse than that moment when you can't be certain he's breathing. Parents can only follow the simple advice given and if tragedy does strike, try not to blame themselves. This is of course easier said than done. Remember:

* Don't put your baby to sleep on her tummy – 'back to bed'.

* Make sure she does not become overheated.
* Do not smoke near a baby.

Nina was constantly disturbed at night by three-week-old Katherine. Between feeds the baby slept fitfully and her mother was becoming exhausted. One night, too tired to sit up to breast-feed Katherine, Nina laid the baby beside her and fed her lying down. Sucking contentedly, the baby soon drifted off to sleep, comforted and peaceful to feel the closeness of her mother. Nina managed to extricate herself and put her back in her own bed, and get some blessed sleep herself.

As soon as possible, babies should become accustomed to being alone at night, or they may develop the habit of wanting to sleep with an adult well into childhood.

COPING WITH CRYING

You will soon recognise the way your baby is crying. Usually it is from hunger, and the very sound can trigger a reflex in the mother who breast-feeds and she feels the milk coming. A certain high-pitched scream will send you racing – she needs you urgently. There are various shades of crying: sobs, winges, whimpers, shouts and screams – you will hear them all.

Sometimes babies cry and it is impossible to work out why. There are few situations as frustrating as this – especially when it happens at the dead of night. But try and be grateful for that sound, it is your child's only way to communicate that he is in need. Some say that babies cry to exercise their lungs, but there is little real evidence that this is ever true. But there must be a reason – he really isn't just doing it to wind you up. It will help to ask yourself the question: *Why is he crying and how can we make him stop?*

1. Is he hungry or thirsty? Maybe milk or some cool boiled water will calm him. If there is a delay before you can deal

with this, perhaps he has got into such a state that beginning to feed him is difficult. Calmly persist, speaking gently and stroking him softly as you encourage him to suck and assuage his appetite.

2. Is he in pain? If so from what? It may be something obvious like something digging into him, but more likely the source of discomfort is on the inside. A frequent activity in babyhood is 'burping'. Before having children this was not something I thought about much, but reckoning up the number of times I have 'brought up wind' in babies over the years, I realise what an important topic it can be.

When a six-year-old gulps down a glass of fizzy lemonade she smiles, waits expectantly and then lets rip a wonderful explosion as the air that was in the drink rises to the top of her stomach and escapes through her mouth. Rather more unmentionable is when the release of air goes downwards rather than up, and most children also have this bodily function down to a fine art, much to our chagrin! In a baby, air enters the stomach while she is screaming, sucking, or even just breathing. When she takes in milk her stomach will feel uncomfortable until she has burped the air-pocket out. Done half-way through the feed in a relaxed manner, bringing up this wind is usually a simple process, but sometimes it isn't so easy. The best way to deal with a 'windy' baby is to hold her gently up against your shoulder, your arm crooked to support the bottom, and give her a few rubs on the back. This operation will sometimes result in her sicking up a bit of milk too, and the resulting whitish stains on the shoulders of all your clothes will be a sort of badge, instantly recognised by other fellow-pilgrims on the path of parenthood! A well-positioned muslin cloth to mop up any regurgitated milk can cut down the washing load and dry-cleaning bills.

Sometimes a baby is suffering from more than this common-or-garden wind and the crying won't stop. You can try a dose of Infacol, lie her on her tummy over your lap while you massage her back, walk about with her on your shoulder, rock her. But the longer it goes on the more tense you both become. It can help to work out a strategy in your mind, you feel less helpless. Something like: 'If this doesn't work by ten past on the clock, I'll try her in the sling. And if she's still screaming then I'll put her in her pram and rock her for a bit while I watch the news, and after that it'll be almost time for the next feed anyway!' Eventually it will stop. The frustrating thing is often never being sure what the problem was in the first place.

Paul and Penny were thrilled to be parents. Young Sean was progressing well, they were beginning to feel life had a kind of order to it and that having babies was quite straightforward after all. Then one evening it started. After his feed, at about five o'clock Sean began to scream. Drawing his legs up to his stomach in pain, this normally easy baby became uncontrollably shaky and impossible to pacify. It went on for two hours. Nothing they tried brought relief for more than a few minutes. The doctor explained that Sean was suffering from colic, and this performance continued every evening at about the same time until he reached three months old.

Nobody has yet found a certain cure for colic, although your health visitor will suggest things you can try; it does not harm the baby and is one of those afflictions that just has to be lived through.

3. Does he feel insecure? For months on end your unborn baby was contained in a warm, soft, alive environment constantly soothed by the rhythmic sounds of his mother's body and the familiar tones of her voice. How different it must be now, out in a bright, changeable world, living as a separate entity no longer attached to his life source. Is it any wonder that babies are more contented and calmer when held close to their mothers or others who know and care for them?

John has an unique method of hushing – I hesitate to say 'calming' – small crying infants. Cupping the head tenderly in one hand and the bottom in the other, he swooshes his daughter backwards and forwards, up and down, fairly fast, imitating, he says, the movement the unborn child would have felt in the womb as his mother walked about. This magically silences her for as long as the action lasts but unfortunately as soon as he stops – it is very energy-consuming – and the babe has regained her wits and breath the wailing begins again. He once demonstrated this technique to a senior health visitor and she politely said she was impressed, and so he has continued the practice with any baby and teaches others about it too.

Justine nearly died when she was born. In the end they only just delivered her in time with high forceps. She had to go on a ventilator straight away and it was a while before the doctor allowed Nat and Helen to have her home. Little Justine never seemed to be happy. Even when she was asleep she'd sometimes twitch and jerk and when she woke up she'd whimper unless someone was holding her. 'We'll spoil her if we pick her up every time she cries,' Helen told her sister. She asked the health visitor about it and as she followed the advice she received life changed dramatically. 'When you put Justine down in her cot, swaddle her. The closeness of the blanket will make her feel safe and she'll sleep much better. And get hold of a baby sling and wear it around the house. She'll love to be in it and you'll soon get used to doing things with your little millstone round your neck!' laughed Sue the health visitor.

One good way to calm a fretful baby is by rocking him. Whether in your arms, lying in a pram, in the baby bouncer or tucked into the baby sling, the rhythm of being rocked often does the trick.

RETURNING TO NORMAL – more or less!

After the birth of your baby it will take many weeks for life to fall into a predictable and manageable pattern. You will devote hours to feeding your baby, and although newborns are meant to sleep several hours each day, perhaps yours is not like that and ties you up for much longer than you had bargained for, just trying to pacify him.

Because your female hormones are still not settled, you may seem emotionally vulnerable and feel the need for extra reassurance and encouragement. Explain this to those close to you, particularly your partner, so that the support you need can be given.

You will react physically and emotionally to childbirth. Your body has been pushed and stretched and battered about through pregnancy and labour. Did you escape stretch marks? There may also be the further physical demand of breast-feeding, the discomfort of stitches and the dawning realisation that the date that for nine months you had been working towards was not the end at all – but a whole new beginning. Most women continue to bleed for about six weeks after their baby's birth and during this time the body begins to return to normal. The feelings of vulnerability may last longer, of course, and some women suffer from postnatal depression (see p. 26).

You will have barely recovered from childbirth, possibly vowing never to repeat the experience, when the doctor will raise the subject of contraception! Probably there is no activity you feel less like just then, however in love you and your mate may be, than intercourse! But the time will come, and it is important then to take precautions to prevent pregnancy. Breast-feeding is *not* reliable as a contraceptive. You may also find that a different method suits you better now: take time out to consult your GP and look into the subject in depth. It is also worth while to think through the ethical and health risk implications of some devices.

Unfortunately, a complete lack of interest in sexual intercourse can often continue for a long time after the birth and lead to strains in your relationship. Many couples may have abstained during the last weeks of the pregnancy, and added to the natural period of postnatal recovery it may seem like an eternity to your partner even if it doesn't to you. The constant physical contact many mothers have with their baby may fulfil the emotional needs previously met by the sexual relationship. Some women find the experience of breast-feeding very satisfying too, and the desire for sexual pleasure is eclipsed by this different but strong enjoyment of a baby. As a new mother, do be careful not to neglect your marital relationship at this time. Starting again after the pregnancy needs care, understanding and tenderness. It may not be easy.

MAKING LOVE AGAIN

Suzanne couldn't bear the thought of making love again. Whether it was the memory of the pain during the labour, that she felt so tired all the time with the baby or an odd sort of anger she felt towards Ed, she didn't know, but it was a big problem between them and talking about it always seemed to cause argument. It was five months now, they'd tried twice but Sue was so tense and it ended in tears and Ed going off to sleep in the spare room. If something didn't happen soon, who could tell where it would end?

This is often a secret problem; you feel a freak, guilty, and the longer it goes on the more impossible the situation can become. Many more couples have experienced times like this than we realise – but it isn't something one can easily talk about.

In most cases time is the answer; the woman's libido will return and the physical side of the relationship can resume. What is important is how you both travel through this trying time of waiting. So many conflicting emotions may arise and things may be said or done which cause misunderstanding, rejection and resentment that can take permanent root in the relationship. Don't be embarrassed to ask for help, this is nothing to feel ashamed of, and recognise that your future happiness may be at stake.

* Be honest with each other about how you feel – but be very careful and gentle in the way you share. Plan this conversation rather than letting it happen as a result of a disagreement.
* Try to understand what your partner needs from you physically. Even if full intercourse is a problem, there are many other ways you can share intimately together. Is the issue primarily a physical one, or are there emotional problems too?
* If possible, find a responsible, caring and understanding person to talk to if the problem is too difficult for you to handle alone.

Life with a newborn feels all-consuming. She needs attention right around the clock but not at first by the clock. Gradually a pattern will emerge and your baby will become a little less the focal point around which every aspect of life has to revolve. Little by little she will twig that there is a difference between day and night – especially if you make the night feeds very quiet, keeping the lights dimmed and spending no time in play with the baby. She will hopefully realise that being awake at night is fairly pointless as little seems to happen. Many babies are very slow to get this message and inflict their parents with broken nights for months or even years. Generally speaking, as the child grows big enough to last longer on each intake of food, you can expect your nights to be less interrupted.

Life may begin to become almost normal.

5

NOBODY'S NORMAL – BUT EVERYONE'S SPECIAL!

'Oh, Bear!' said Christopher Robin. 'How I do love you!'
'So do I,' said Pooh.

Winnie-the-Pooh, A. A. Milne

The starting point for every parent in every aspect of raising children must always be love. Even if it is not always easy, try to accept a child just the way he is, not allowing feelings of disappointment or criticism to cloud our unconditional commitment to protect, care and raise him to be the person he was destined to be.

WATCHING THEM GROW

It is fascinating for parents to watch their children develop. Year by year, month by month, even from one day to the next, they acquire new skills. Their personalities mature and we see the changes in the way our children move, use their hands and relate to the world around them.

There are some charts at the end of this book highlighting landmarks and milestones of children's development during the first four years. These will give you a idea of what to expect. But *please* don't regard these guidelines as necessary goals for your child to achieve. No boy or girl is likely to fit exactly into such a formula. Your toddler may be flummoxed about putting on her socks but confident to name perhaps a dozen colours. Perhaps the baby isn't pushing himself up with his arms at the age the experts say is normal. Your daughter is still not walking at eighteen months but had four or five recognisable words well before her first birthday. Everybody is different and we all develop according to our unique timetables.

Most children have some problem as they grow, whether temporary or permanent, and although it is natural to be concerned if everything isn't going 'by the book', try not to worry – many of our fears turn out to be groundless. If not, much can usually be done to enable your child to cope with their disability – whether it is minor or serious. You will find the regular development checks carried out by your GP or health visitor reassuring and helpful.

INOCULATIONS AND DEVELOPMENT CHECKS

When you registered your baby with your family doctor, his or her name should have been added to the local Health District's computerised list. In theory, this means you will be automatically notified when health and development checks are due and also when to take your child for those vitally important vaccinations. However, even computers 'forget', so it is wise to check up yourself so that nothing is missed. Health Authorities may differ from each other and new procedures are brought in from time to time, but your GP or health visitor will be glad to give you the latest information. They will tell you about the timing of both these all-important inoculations and also the health checks that will take place regularly during your child's first four years.

Immunisations

Your baby needs to be protected from a variety of diseases. Many illnesses have been almost eradicated in this country because of the mass immunisation programme for young children, but unless each course is completed they will not be effective. Some babies become a little unwell after their inoculations but this is not serious and should only last a day or so. Do not take your baby to a swimming pool until at least three weeks following the third immunisations of her first series, by which time she will be about five months old.

TEETH

First teeth begin to appear from about six months on but dental care begins from birth by avoiding sweet drinks. Fluoride is now added to our water in order to reduce tooth decay. The amount varies from one area to another and if children have too much fluoride, it can make their teeth brown. Ask your dentist to advise you. He will recommend the best kind of toothpaste for you to use for your baby. From the age of about three take your child to the dentist – at first just to become accustomed to the idea.

The routine of cleaning teeth can be introduced as soon as there are any. The best way to encourage brushing is by offering a small, soft toothbrush to be played with – especially after a meal or in the bath. Don't bother with toothpaste at first, and then just a smear.

Sugar rots teeth, so the less children have, the better. Offer a piece of carrot or apple instead of a biscuit and choose fruit juices and infant rusks with low sugar content; always avoid sweetened milk and fruit cordials. Check the ingredients of any baby food you buy, and encourage your baby to enjoy a varied diet.

Teething can be blamed for almost any ailment in babies! Some sprout molars, incisors and canines with the greatest of ease. A very few (Napoleon is one example) are born with theirs already in place! Most babies experience mild discomfort, and a few are troubled with pain as the teeth come through.

* Painful gums may make the baby more dribbly than usual. A towelling bib round his neck can mop up the drips.

* The soreness will probably make your baby grizzly. Reach for the Calpol (paracetamol syrup) – carefully noting recommended dosages – and ask your pharmacist for a soothing gel to rub into the gums. Hard toys, special teething rings, and pieces of raw carrot to chew all help you, and the troublesome tooth, through.
* Teething sometimes causes mild diarrhoea and the baby's feeding patterns may change for a while. This is nothing to worry about.

EYES AND EARS

Needless to say, it is most important to check if you have any concerns about your baby's ears or eyes. If her eyes are a bit 'sticky', gently bathe with warm water on a cotton bud – it should clear up quickly. If it does not, your health visitor or GP may prescribe other treatment. If you think your child is squinting, have this checked too; it may have to be followed up. The developmental checks already described will routinely monitor sight and hearing. Unless your doctor advises it, there is no need to visit an optician until your child is much older.

Sometimes small children pick up an ear infection, especially following a cold. Unfortunately babies cannot alert you to this, but poor sleeping and feeding, with restless, miserable behaviour, may. The outside of the ear may feel hot. Your doctor will be able to look inside the ear and may prescribe an antibiotic.

When should you visit the doctor? Whenever you are concerned; a sympathetic family doctor prefers a few false alarms to being called out later to an emergency! She will agree to see a young child without an appointment if you are genuinely worried. As time goes on you will feel more confident to judge whether or not your child is ill and will have learned how to help him get better. Find out what services are available at your surgery. Is it possible to speak to your GP on the telephone at certain times of the day?

Does she run a 'well baby clinic' (which is of course for unwell babies too)?

CHILDREN WITH SPECIAL NEEDS

Although it is helpful to have benchmarks to measure development, no child is 'normal'! We are all advantaged and disadvantaged in different areas, so you will make both positive and problematic discoveries about your child as time goes on. If he has specific needs or suffers from a serious condition, try not to compare your youngster's progress with other children who appear to be disconcertingly healthy and forward! Yours will probably get there in the end! – and in five years' time it won't matter that he was months late in crawling or speaking clearly.

When she was six weeks old, Tara was diagnosed as having a rare syndrome and likely to experience considerable problems. The use of her ears, eyes, half her insides, the ability to develop physically and mentally were all in question. The situation turned out to be much brighter than at first feared – but those early weeks of uncertainty and worry were very difficult for her family. She needed plenty of extra love and care; in her first year there were more than fifty doctor's appointments and she was late in reaching many developmental milestones. Tara grew into a delightful and very intelligent child. Despite her partial sight, she attended the nursery class of a normal primary school when she was three and with the help of a special care assistant had, by the age of ten, more than caught up with her peers.

Richard, whose story began in chapter 3, has cystic fibrosis. His parents described how they have coped with caring for him. He is five now and doing well but this inherited disease affects the mucous linings of the body, and the main problems occur in the intestines and the chest. CF is a terminal illness, although the life expectancy of sufferers is lengthening and treatment is becoming more and more successful. Right through babyhood Richard took more than seventy tablets a day, needed regular physiotherapy morning and night and was prone to any bugs that were passing by. 'When they told us, I cried and so much wanted it not to be true,' said Patricia. 'I didn't know how long he would live or what it would mean to our lives. We felt we had Richard on loan and one day he would be taken away from us – we still do to a certain extent.'

One of the hardest things to handle is having to share your baby with the medical profession. 'Of course we all depend on and deeply appreciate the expertise and concern doctors have for our special child, but when we enter the clinic, somehow he is less Richard and more a cystic fibrosis case. Parenting is seen primarily as "managing the disease".'

As parents it is crucial to develop good, trusting relationships with all the professionals you deal with.

* Contact any specialist group to help you understand and receive support about your child's condition.
* Make an appointment to explain the situation to your GP and make sure he is willing to take your child on – especially if it is a fund-holding practice.
* Keep a file – ask for photocopies of any reports about your child, make notes about discussions, test results and treatments. Be pro-active as a parent!
* Write a journal to record how you feel and the important milestones and happenings, how the rest of the family copes with the ongoing situation.

Patricia and Andy had to break the news about their baby to family and friends. Andy was keen to tell people over the phone. Patricia could not face it and managed to write a letter to go out with Richard's birth announcement.

It is agonising for parents to be in a situation like this, and if you are facing something similar you will know the loneliness, fears and sense of guilt and failure which can come at your lowest moments, and yet the incalculable rewards that also come. These special children need extra attention, and caring for them can be draining and demanding. Attending yet another appointment at the clinic or hospital and having to face again the verdicts of the medical profession will get you down and cause you to wonder about the future.

It is crucially important to find people who can support you – preferably other parents who have had similar experiences and can reassure and advise you. There are hundreds of groups set up to help parents with children suffering from specific conditions. Get in touch as soon as you can. Family and friends will also hopefully be there for you and perhaps you will discover a local church that will offer friendship and meet your very important spiritual needs in this situation.

Accept your child just as she is but at the same time motivate her all along the way. Never give up helping her to achieve her potential. Guide and encourage her without pressure, and try not to show anxiety or disappointment at her shortcomings. Let her know she's absolutely brilliant!

We all long to be accepted and loved just for who we are – not for what we ought to be. From babyhood on, let your children know you are crazy about them because they are themselves – not because of their successes or looks. Be straightforward in explaining that they are different as soon as they begin to realise it. 'You need to have this medicine because you have cystic fibrosis', may seem rather blunt, but it is a truth Richard has to come to terms with for the rest of his life. Caring for children with disabilities or other difficulties is no picnic and so you should seek out all the support, advice and help you need, different at each stage of the journey; from family, friends, medical and educational professionals, so that the best can be done for you as a family.

PART TWO
EIGHTEEN MONTHS
TO FOUR YEARS

6
WHAT PARENTING
IS *REALLY* LIKE!

Parenting isn't for cowards

Dr James Dobson

For years we were unashamedly avid fans of *Little House on the Prairie*. Week by week the whole family would gather round the television to enjoy the latest adventures of the Ingalls family. My favourite character was Carolyn, the mother I could never be in a hundred years, always immaculate in her starched white apron and not a hair out of place. This woman spent her days solving crises, baking pies, teaching children, cleaning, mending, soothing sick babies and always smiled through it all. I wanted to be like that, but kept telling myself she lived her blameless life on a film set, not in real life. Surely nobody could really be as perfect as Carolyn.

Most of us have our idealised visions of parenthood, maybe gleaned from the past, from stories or just our own imagination. There is nothing wrong with that – so long as when reality strikes we don't feel depressed because it doesn't turn out as we dreamed.

WEEKEND BLUES

'I absolutely adore my kids, but looking after them sometimes drives me crazy!' my friend Fiona confessed.

I'd hazard a guess that most of us have felt the same way some time or other. Looking after little children is unbelievably labour-intensive, from the process of birth onwards. There is never a holiday – babies need the same things without fail seven days a week. Weekends are no longer the well-earned days away from work or study that they used to be. Mothers often unconsciously suffer from the 'weekend blues'. From an early age we have been taught that weekends are special, because once the necessary chores are out of the way, there is usually time to do something for fun – different from the rest of the week. For older children, Saturdays may mean horse riding, football or just hanging around the house. For the average teenager they are the chance for a lie-in, and the man of the house may enjoy pottering about the garden, a spot of DIY, or even a couple of hours enjoying his favourite armchair sporting event.

But for us mothers, Saturdays are in danger of being just like other days of the week – or even worse because nobody leaves you in peace to get on – and very often there seems no respite from the monotony of the menial tasks associated with running a home and caring for little ones. This can seriously get you down, so what about some kind of strategy to beat 'Mum's weekend blues'?

1. Set aside time on Friday to plan and prepare for the weekend. Decide what you'll eat and maybe cook some things ready. Check that the laundry basket is emptyish and that no urgent ironing will be needed during the weekend.
2. Negotiate a lie-in and/or breakfast brought to you in bed. Your partner may welcome the opportunity to see to the squalling, soggy baby for a change – you never know.
3. Make the best use of the hours when your children are safely ensconsed in bed rather than let the time disappear.
4. Try to go out together as a family, for a walk, to the playground or the swimming pool.
5. If Sunday involves a busy schedule and cooking a family meal, spend an hour the evening before preparing vegetables, getting clothes together if you haven't done that

already on Friday and laying the breakfast table. You'll feel better for it and Sunday may be more restful as a result.
6. Make wise use of your television set – or even better a video cassette recorder. Record suitable programmes for your two- to four-year-olds earlier in the week; even ones they've watched already will entertain them for half an hour or more while you relax.

FITTING EVERYTHING IN

However, if you are in employment outside the home, working to keep your family on your own or supplementing your partner's income, this relaxing regime is less than a joke. For you Saturday will mean cleaning, washing and ironing as well as caring for the family. It is vital for you to find some leisure time each week. Perhaps there is another day when you could take a bit of time to yourself and accept that the weekend is probably too busy.

My friend Terrie is amazing. She runs a playgroup in term time, looks after various children in the afternoons as well as being kept busy raising her own family of six children, two of them pre-school age. Looking at Terrie with young children, it is obvious that she has a natural way with kids. Surrounded by babies and toddlers who seem automatically attracted to her, even when chaos surrounds her she always has an air of serenity that astonishes me.

Fiona and her husband waited several years to start a family, during which time Fiona worked hard at her career in magazine publishing. The total shock of motherhood completely threw her. Although as the pregnancy progressed Fiona wound down her work with a view to taking a couple of years out to devote to the new baby, she was unprepared for the radical change of lifestyle. The initial excitement of going to the weekly baby clinic with her son soon wore off, as did being at home day by day. Finally she and her husband decided to employ a nanny so Fiona could return to work.

Most of us would identify ourselves as being somewhere in between Terrie and Fiona. We all need to be aware of our gifts and our shortcomings, but to stop feeling inadequate or a failure because we are not the same sort of mother as someone else. Perhaps you haven't a clue how to look after babies and the prospect is quite daunting. How will you know the right thing to do? Do you see yourself as a 'natural' mother or absolutely useless with children? These nagging doubts are sure to come – especially if up until now you have had little to do with babies.

Don't panic! Continue to be yourself, simply expressing who you are through a different role. Your babies don't need super-efficient, wonderfully creative, temperamentally perfect parents. You will do nicely as you set about learning new skills, and loving them the best you can *is* enough. There is no such person as Supermum. She's as much a myth as the Tooth Fairy or Father Christmas. Parents who are bringing up children alone need to hear this message more than any of us. It is not possible to be father and mother, supporter, provider, teacher and playmate on your own, so don't attempt the impossible and feel a miserable failure when you run out of steam.

Ed's wife died after a long, painful illness, leaving him to raise their three children. The youngest was only six months old. He told me:

> I despaired. How could I look after them on my own and ever replace the mother they had lost? One day at a time we lived, kept sane through the support of friends and family. I realised that our family life would always have its limitations and there was only so much I could do or be. We made it, but it was never very easy.

A PARENTS' CHARTER

1. *Make sure you are showing your child lots of physical affection.* This may be harder if you are an undemonstrative

person and you will need to develop the habit of hugging, kissing, playing and tickling your baby, looking into her face and telling her you love her. All of us need to feel a sense of security, self-worth and significance. Toddlers are no exception.

2. *Be willing to learn how to care for your child.* There's plenty of advice around. Listen to it and decide what is right for you. Different people have different approaches. Don't take everyone's advice – you'll only get confused! Decide whose judgment you trust, and combine that with what you think best yourself.

3. *Be honest about your weaknesses and try to get around them.* If, for example, you can't face the thought of toddlers, paint and glue in your kitchen, take them to a Mother and Toddler group or One O'Clock Club where this messy activity is all laid on. They can slosh and splosh to their hearts' content, leaving your home unvandalised.

4. *Make space for yourself.* The woman who can accept the inevitable restrictions of motherhood but also salvage some time for personal pleasure and relaxation will enjoy her small children more. There are times when the future seems to stretch ahead like an endless life-sentence of fractious infants, broken nights and messy clutter. But there *will* come a day when you no longer pack a spare nappy in your handbag and sing nursery rhymes as you walk along the street.

5. *Enjoy your child.* Find out how you can teach your baby new skills and enjoy being part of her growing up. Don't wish this time away – you may look back with pangs of regret at what later look like the golden days.

6. *Say a prayer* for your children even if this is something new to you. The birth of a baby often activates a spiritual response and makes us think through some important issues. You may find a nearby church which seems friendly and ready to share the Christian faith with you and your child. See if it runs any special events or groups. And at home, when that darling infant finally *does* go to sleep, why

not ask God to protect him, help him grow to maturity and reach his potential?

7. If you are married, *take care of your relationship*. Even though small children demand your full attention, energy and emotional involvement, it is dangerous to neglect the first relationship of family life – with your partner. You must find ways to spend enough time together to talk, listen and share – and once your body is back in full working order, to re-establish your sexual relationship. The greatest gift parents can bestow upon children is their love for each other! Otherwise insecurity and discord may filter down into children's subconscious minds and sow seeds of unhappiness in their lives.

'TAKE ME AWAY FROM ALL THIS!'

With so much of life revolving round the next feed and the price of nappies, fathers would be very well advised to find ways of distracting the new mother by sometimes whisking her away to something completely different. A film, a relaxed meal, even a cup of coffee in a cafe would be a good break. But do not be surprised if the prospect of leaving a young baby proves too much for her. Be patient and try to understand the insecurity she feels. 'What if she cries?' may seem an insignificant fear to you, but the sense of responsibility, the feeling of inadequacy and guilt if she isn't being 'a good mother' are very real and experienced by most first-time mums. The tie is a strong physical bond still, and you need to be gentle as you help her to take up her own identity and life again, along with the new role your child demands of her.

7
SO, HOW WAS YOUR DAY?

Today I walked one mile and ran at least two
performed three emergency rescues and four
minor operations
answered questions on natural history, mechanics,
astronomy and religion
acted as nursemaid, chauffeur, housekeeper,
cook and freelance entertainer.
Today I was your mother

The Gift of a Child, Marion Stroud

Dawn comes at ten to five. Mingling with the music of blackbirds and robins singing joyously in the dew-washed gardens of Manchester is another sound which penetrates sleep . . . the frenzied shriek of an eighteen-month-old child, screaming frantically. There is no way of ignoring him, so with a sigh Janet gets up to investigate what is clearly a major emergency. But behold! As she enters his room the noise miraculously ceases and a radiant smile appears on his teary, scarlet face. He leaps up and down in his cot, sucking a disgustingly soggy comfort blanket and reaches out to his beloved gleefully.

Down in the kitchen Janet makes a hot drink for herself and a warm one for him and they gulp it companionably together. As she tries to recover from her rude awakening, Alistair peers at her teeth and pokes inside her mouth with a plastic spoon like a trainee dentist. Another day of parenthood has begun.

A MOTHER'S LOT

Sharing life with babies and toddlers demands a special brand of unselfishness which few of us naturally possess. Many women would say that mothering is unequivocally the most challenging and difficult task they have ever undertaken. You may have previously worked as a high-powered professional and now sometimes look wistfully at the dusty brief-case you used to carry to the job 'BC' – before children. This is a strategic moment to count the blessings of parenthood.

A friend of ours – with two young children and a very understanding husband! – once received a little gift from him. It was a small, elegant box of a hundred gold-edged business cards bearing their address, telephone number and the office fax number, and under her name the words 'Director of Social Development'. Fed up with often being described as 'just a housewife' she really appreciated the gesture and enjoyed using the cards.

Harriet, formerly an actress, was fed up. People at the parties she and her husband often attended in connection with his job seemed to live on a separate planet from her rumble-tumble existence happily at home with three-year-old twins and a teenage foster daughter. She felt belittled by the glamorous women with their unbelievably perfect hair and nail polish and had had enough of bemused reactions when she explained she was at home, looking after the children. One evening she tried a new angle. 'My job? Well it's fascinating! Never a dull moment! Quite a lot of travelling (to playgrounds); constant interaction with people (mostly manic toddlers); therapy and psychological counselling (all ages); basic health care and personal development, creative and educational activites. I do quite a bit of entertaining too (fish fingers and oven chips) and basically manage a residential complex (or complex residence). Of course there's a lot of overtime ... But that's enough of boring old me. What do *you* do?'

'Oh!' came the subdued reply, 'I'm only an international model.'

LABOUR OF LOVE

It is not unusual to feel undervalued and isolated as a mother of small children. The days are filled with hundreds of insignificant-seeming tasks, demanding infants and mess. The most stimulating conversation is often non-stop interaction with a three-year-old whose favourite word is 'Why?' and maybe a chat about the price of carrots with the greengrocer. Your clothes are usually stained with anything and everything your baby manages to smear on you, and your home will frequently resemble the aftermath of a major hurricane.

In any family, a considerable amount of thought, time and energy goes into producing food. Once your baby has passed the stage when she lived on milk only, the issue of feeding becomes a major one. There are various alternatives when it comes to food preparation and presentation – and a number of pitfalls that are best avoided.

* Wean your baby on to solid food gradually. If the first response to your painstakingly pureed potato is to spit it out, try not to take it personally.
* Weigh up the advantages and disadvantages of using commercially produced baby and toddler food. It's convenient, contains the necessary nutrients, is quick to prepare and portable, but on the other hand stuff in packets, tins or jars is expensive and if your child becomes used to their rather bland taste he may not take to home-cooked food later.
* Don't become anxious about eating. Your baby will pick up your concerns and may not be as relaxed or amenable at mealtimes as you would like. Unless he has some illness, the baby will not starve. Offer a variety of finger foods as well as the spoon-it-in variety. He will almost certainly eat the items he needs.

* Keep away from sugary or salty processed food as much as possible. Give him baby rusks rather than ordinary biscuits, dilute fruit juices and keep chocolate and sweets from him as long as you can. (This will not work if you have older children in the home already.) Pieces of fruit, salad and raw carrot are wonderful – although many babies suss out that you really want them to eat food like this because it's healthy and therefore reject it.

* Many toddlers and small children are faddy about eating. Trying to get food down a reluctant three-year-old can be exhausting. Make sure a child like this is hungry – watch those in-between snacks – and try to give only the amount you are sure he will easily eat. It is much better to empty a plate with less on it than to eat the same amount but fail to finish. You can try games, but be careful these do not become totally necessary to lever the tiniest baked bean down his reluctant throat.

* If you want to increase his intake of fruit, try handing him a piece as he sits in his pushchair or watches his favourite video. Putting food in pretty little dishes, or a special lunch box, may encourage enjoyable eating.

* Be firm when your toddler is playing about with his food. Try to insist on the first course being finished if he is to have pudding. Encourage good manners – have a few rules about staying at the table until he is finished, food staying on the dish, not on the floor, and saying thank you at the end.

There will still be the occasional tantrum as he rejects the food you have so lovingly prepared. It's all part of an average day's work.

Somehow we must find the balance between attending to the needs of a young child or children, meeting the other responsibilities that fall to us, maintaining relationships with family and friends and yet finding some space for ourselves. This sounds obvious enough, but most days it's totally unrealistic.

Women and men who parent alone are particularly vulnerable when their children are small, often suffering loneliness and anxiety about the future as well as having too much to do.

In some ways it is easier to raise a younger child with older siblings who has to fit into an already existing routine. Even if he has not finished breakfast, is still in his sleepsuit and happens to be throwing a tantrum, the school run must go on and he comes too! Attitudes are more relaxed and you are not so anxious about doing everything 'right'.

But when Dave and Pat's two children were at the toddler stage with just eighteen months difference in their ages it felt very different. They also had a new baby. At times Pat was overwhelmed by the never-ending demands and seemed to achieve very little each day. Often still in her dressing gown by mid-morning (even though she had been up and doing since six), even the simplest of tasks like getting washed and dressed or writing a shopping list were interrupted and left unfinished. On the whole life was fun and she and Dave look back with very happy memories, but everything seemed quite a struggle and by the end of some days these parents were completely exhausted, frustrated and wondering if they were winning.

Managing small children is made far easier when life has some kind of order in it.

DON'T TAKE LIFE TOO SERIOUSLY

A sense of humour is absolutely super-essential. The annoyance you feel at a child's repeated misdemeanours is so understandable. Eva's daughter was quiet upstairs (ominous) and it turned out that little Hilary had carefully unravelled an entire multi-pack of toilet rolls – Scottex puppy style. 'I didn't know whether to scream, shout or laugh – by the time I found her she was trying to eat the tissues and then spitting them out in disgust!' There is a choice here – you can reach for the camera and smile or lose your cool. On occasions like this, some days you'll do the first, but on others the funny side will elude you and you'll angrily pluck her up in your arms and maybe even shout! But don't take your baby's sins too seriously; life is too short.

PLAN AHEAD

Although it may seem to go against the grain to do boring tasks before they are absolutely necessary, you will never regret doing things early. Even if you are by nature a procrastinator, do try to organise yourself. It will maximise precious time, lessen the stress level and help you not to forget vital details. Part of your daily routine can be to put out a bundle of clothes for each child for the next day, get most of the food preparation for tea, supper and tomorrow's school packed lunches out of the way in the first part of the day and put washed breakfast dishes straight back on a tray ready to lay up for the next morning before the end of the day. (This only works if you have a lot of toddlerproof surfaces.) Try to do birthday cards before the last minute to save that frantic sprint with the double buggy to the post office to catch the last post. Try making lists – it feels so good when you can cross jobs off when they're done. You should also add the other things that weren't on the original list but you did anyway, for the joy of ticking them off and making the catalogue of activities look longer. Life is full enough of surprises without needing to be caught out by the things which we know will happen.

TAKE TIME TO BE YOU

Getting washed and dressed first thing in the morning may not seem such an extraordinary feat to a person who does not have small children. After all, everyone does it – what's the problem? Aha! Even if it means leaving your baby grumbling in his cot perfuming the entire house with an aromatic nappy, he can wait until you have your clothes on! (This also means it is wise to make your own little clothes bundle the day before as well!) And if you can actually manage to creep downstairs before he even wakes, to have a cup of tea and a couple of minutes of peace to yourself . . . the morning is off to a decidedly hopeful start. Once the demands begin, it is very difficult to snatch time to get ready for the day. Even if your children have rests or go to playgroup there are a thousand and one jobs to do around the house. They never all get done. Make it a priority to grab a break if you possibly can, and make sure the evening has a cut-off point, when you and your partner can both relax together. Aim to have everyone in bed before your favourite programme starts. This may not be possible if your babies and children are difficult to settle and have sleep problems. And you may prefer a later start in the morning; seven o'clock bedtime may mean an unwelcome six a.m. alarm call.

Pauline goes to keep fit classes at the local leisure centre and also a pottery class at the adult education institute. Both these run a creche and her two toddlers enjoy the break as much as she does. 'The opportunity to do something just for me does me a world of good. I completely forget they exist sometimes when I'm engrossed in what I'm doing. Then we have a cheap lunch in the cafeteria and that's a real treat too. '

ROUTINE

Divide up the day into manageable sections. At six in the morning the hours ahead can seem endless. Routines and regularity can really help. This is how Pat described a typical day with Becky aged three-and-a-half, Harry, two, and four-month-old Simon.

About 6.00   Simon wakes for a feed. Go downstairs, put him in his bouncer with a rusk and make tea. Put out milk and cereals and tidy the remains of last night's meal. Carefully carry baby and tea back to bed and wake husband Dave. Breast-feed Simon.

6.30   Commotion next door informs us the others are up and bouncing. Dave goes in to sort them out with drinks of juice.

7.00   Baby back down to sleep. We all get ready chaotically.

7.30   Breakfast. Dave kisses us all fondly and makes his escape!

8–9.30   Clearing up. Children playing nearby. Put on a wash, get things ready to go out. Get Simon back up, feed him again. Leave to take Becky to playgroup.

10.00   Do a bit of shopping on the way home.

10.30   Mid-morning drink and biscuit. Read Harry a book or two and settle him to do more reading/puzzles/drawing/making.

11–12.00   Baby asleep, work in kitchen getting lunch, etc.

12.30 Playgroup finishes

1.00   Lunch – including feeding Simon.

1.40   Becky and Harry watch children's TV, then Harry has nap while I wash up. Simon sits in his bouncer. Quick coffee while I make some phone calls and open the post.

2.30   Start getting ready to go out. Put things for tea and night clothes in bathroom ready. Wake Harry.

3.00   Out to park, One O'Clock Club or to a friend.

4.00   Simon needs feeding again and the others want a drink and a biscuit.

4.30–5.00   Home. Bath the older ones then give them tea. Bedtime story.

6.30   Lights out. Get Simon ready for bed, feed him and put him down by 7.30 by which time Dave's back.

8.00   Eat our supper. I feel shattered!

Anyone who thinks staying home and looking after young children is a soft option should try it for a day! In between time- and energy-consuming child care there are all the chores of shopping, ironing, cooking and cleaning to fit in too. Many fathers are brilliant at shouldering the domestic load and take their share of some of these responsibilities. Others need gentle encouragement to do a bit more.

Maybe a routine like this looks too structured for your liking but make a start and at least have definite times for lunch, tea and bed. It isn't easy to gauge how long everything will take at first, but keep at it. Children prefer a sense of pattern in their lives and so long as the regime is flexible you will find it helpful too.

GOING OUT

It helps to be a bit of an outdoor person when you are the parent of under-fives.

Mark and Cathy have three small children and often go out together as a family. By tramping through the local common or countryside, swimming at the local leisure centre, lugging bikes and trikes to the park or just going to the swings, the family comes home exhausted, famished and rosy-cheeked. The house is still reasonably tidy and they have been together. Come rain or shine, on a Sunday afternoon when the lure of sport on the TV is strong, Mark still gets his family out and really enjoys it.

Fathers who can do this are contributing so much to their children's experience and they will understand more of what life in the raw is like for mothers!

Kirsty and her twin girls have a full programme. Living in an area where there is plenty to choose from they can do something different every afternoon of the week.

* Monday – Swimming (free at certain times at her local pool or at the special Mother and Baby sessions).

* Tuesday – Library (story time is at 2.30. Her two children listen while she hunts for books).
* Wednesday – a local 'Mums and Toddlers' group where she meets friends over a cup of tea while her daughters play.
* Thursday – One O'Clock Club.
* Friday – Roly-Poly Club (Inflatables in a local hall).

None of these costs much – if anything – and it really helps to escape from home for a few hours.

Going out every day does all of you good; the children don't get bored, you have a change of scenery, you might meet some interesting people and the house doesn't get messed up. Even the simplest expedition can be made fun and takes quite a chunk from a long day at home.

POOLING RESOURCES

Do not try to do everything alone. Some days children drive you crazy. As a mother, you will soon discover that being ill is off limits. If you wake up feeling 'fluey you most often just have to cope with it. Even the most wonderful father is unlikely to be able to take a day off to help, and if you do not have others to support you it can be a problem. Gather a network of other mums together who are willing to help each other. One day you can leave your child with a friend. She will have a free day next week in exchange when you mind her son. And two compatible children can be easier than a lone bored, discontented one.

Jess and Ali live five doors away from each other. Between them they have one set of twins (two-and-a-half), a three-year-old, a baby and an energetic labrador. They have an excellent co-operative system. In the next street Maureen, pregnant and with a two-year-old son, also joins in from time to time. Ali explains:

We take turns to cook the lunch, alternate days. If one of us is going shopping, the other minds the kids. We go to the park together and keep each other company – we have a good laugh sometimes; it really stops us from getting down. One day my twins were driving me crazy. They were both wingeing, I wasn't well and felt like screaming. I grabbed them and ran down the road to Jess. 'Here you are! Take them before I do them an injury,' I begged her, and ran home and slept for two hours!

When one child has a doctor's appointment, she can go alone with her parent while the other children stay behind. And at times of crisis Jess and Ali find they really depend on each other and wonder how they would cope alone.

A father can be the backbone of any family. Most men come home tired after a demanding day working outside the home. In days gone by they may have expected to put their feet up until supper was on the table and enjoy the ministrations of their wives, looking attractive and ready to provide pleasant companionship and maybe later a night of passion and romance! Is this realistic? For women out at work all day who then return home to another full-time job – being a mother – it is no joke to have an unsupportive partner.

Parenthood should be a partnership. It is not easy to be single-handed, although increasingly many have to, and succeed in raising lovely children on their own.

Finally, draw back and remember to look at life through the eyes of a baby more often. The games of 'Peep-Bo', tickles, and squishing jelly in your fingers belong to a particularly messy part of life which at times we may wish would hurry up and pass! Don't be embarrassed to enjoy your child. His excitement at seeing a bus or being put in his buggy for a walk, being bathed or allowed to crawl through the back garden, is precious and the baby will soon be gone, leaving you with memories and hopefully few regrets.

8

ENTERTAINING TODDLERS

My naughty little sister was a very, very inquisitive
child. She was always looking and peeping into things
that didn't belong to her.
My Naughty Little Sister Stories, Dorothy Edwards

While the demands of babyhood focus on sleeping, feeding
and crying, perhaps the major characteristic of toddler care
is managing the extraordinary amount of mess they can
cause! Aside from the common or garden messes caused by
spilt cereal, muddy footprints and upturned toy boxes, each
day brings a dozen or so major mop up jobs around the
place.

THE MESSY YEARS

One particular morning it took longer than usual for Amy
to make the early morning tea because a two-and-a-half
year old was assisting. Eager to join in, and discovering
that yesterday afternoon's dregs were still in the teapot,
he helpfully poured them out. Cold tea swamped the
worktop, behind and underneath all the items on it,
and best of all overflowed into the cutlery drawer be-
low, to dribble down to the floor.

This accident added to her youngster's repertoire – he
was once caught brushing his teeth with the loo brush, the
contents of the sandpit would be occasionally smuggled in
through the back door and 'cooked'. He also loved colour –
applying it to things like walls, with lipstick or felt tip pens.

And although by two his table manners were showing signs of improvement, he had a few unfortunate lapses like the time he tipped his bowl of spaghetti bolognese over his sister's freshly shampooed head.

You will experience your own unique mess syndrome if you have anyone between the ages of one and about three residing in your home! An inquisitive toddler can wreak untold damage on the average environment, so make certain never to leave your child unattended unless you are quite sure everything is secure. Apart from the mess, there is always a safety risk involved.

By the end of an average day, when your toddler is besmeared with jam, paint, mud and worse, the ritual of bath time can be an enormous relief. The lovely warm, sweet-smelling person who emerges from the bubbles may restore your good humour. As he giggles, hiding in the towel and says 'Boo!' to the currently favoured soft toy, maybe you can forget about the chaos he has caused during the last twelve hours. Tomorrow will be filled with new discoveries and messy adventures, but for now you're nearly through and with any luck you can get him down in his cot in time to catch the latest episode of your favourite TV or radio programme. However much you adore your children, there is an exquisite feeling as the last goodnight and firmly closed door heralds a few hours without them!

HAPPILY OCCUPIED

An inexperienced father kindly offered to look after his two young daughters (eighteen months and three years) one Saturday morning to give his wife a break. He had always wondered what the fuss was about – surely watching a couple of kids was an easy day's work? By the time she returned, the household was upside-down, the children crying and her husband distraught and repentant of his earlier opinion.

Taking care of small children is an extremely difficult and demanding occupation for which this well-meaning husband was totally unprepared. And if it isn't challenging enough to mind the children all day and every day there are always endless housekeeping jobs to be done at the same time, not to mention any other responsibilities and commitments.

A key to sanity in this situation is for the children to be happy and occupied. The answer is not just to provide lots of toys and books, although these are invaluable, because expecting young children to be able to entertain themselves is not always reasonable. But if you can teach them ways to occupy their time, it will pay great dividends in terms of future peace and quiet. Half an hour of your undivided attention now, introducing a child to a new book/puzzle/toy, should buy you some time to do other things uninterrupted later. So how can we keep them gainfully busy?

TOYS

There is an unbelievable selection of toys available for under-fours, and some of them seem to cost an unbelievably large amount of money! Don't go overboard – young children often prefer playing with your wooden spoons and plastic containers to the latest super-educational gizmo. Here are some points to bear in mind as you consider the best items to choose for your child.

* Try to buy good quality items which will satisfy them for a good length of time without falling apart. Check for safety.
* If you can avoid it, do not go to the toyshop with a toddler or small child – it can bring out the worst in them and you may be railroaded into unwise purchases.
* Look for sources of second-hand toys – especially larger items – and save yourself money.

* Consider making a list of suggestions to circulate at Christmas and birthday times. That way your child will receive gifts you really know he will use and like.

* Choose a balance of toys that will stimulate your child. Large and small, moving and still, noisy and quiet, different textures and uses. Spend time showing him how to enjoy them.

* Ring the changes. If certain toys are unavailable for a few weeks and then re-introduced they receive more attention than if they are always there and are taken for granted.

* Keep a collection that only comes out in certain circumstances – on a long journey or when a child is unwell.

* Teach your child about tidying up right from baby-hood. It can become a game and early training will pay dividends later on.

SOME SUGGESTIONS

Young babies:

* Mobiles – especially wind-up musical ones.

* Rattles and other hard, suckable, shakable, squeezable objects.

* Play mat with interesting textures and items sewn into it.

* Cuddly toys – usually bought by adults who cannot resist them!

* Toys that attach to a pram or push-chair.

Crawling babies:

* Your child will continue to enjoy playing with the toys she already has for some months.

* Floor toys like spinning tops, toys on wheels, large blocks and interlocking bricks (like Duplo).

* A baby-walker (she sits in it and moves it with her feet).

* Walking trolley with bricks.

Toddlers:
* Construction bricks.
* Pull-along toys.
* Trundle tricycle – without pedals.
* Sit-on wheeled toys.
* Sand-pit.
* Collections of cars, dolls, etc – for both sexes.
* Very simple puzzles, shapes-posting toy.

Pre-school children:
* Tricycle with pedals, wheelbarrow, etc.
* Climbing frame.
* Small trampoline.
* Pretend toys – farm, dolls' house, etc.
* Dressing-up clothes, hats, bags and other props. (A few bought outfits are a very good investment.)
* Puzzles.
* Play-dough, drawing, painting equipment.
* Cassette player for story and song tapes.

THE TREASURE OF BOOKS

Maybe even more important than providing suitable toys is introducing a child to books. Even very young ones can enjoy them and a lifelong habit of reading can begin very early on. Some children are more into books than others but even so, with encouragement you can tie up hours with productive 'bookery'.

New ideas, shapes, bright colours, interesting people, crazy animals, extraordinary contraptions, are there on the pages to enter his mind and stimulate his thoughts. Even the texture of the pages, the lovely smell of new shiny covers, add to the immediate experience of 'reading'. Early books should have clear, simple pictures of familiar objects and people. You can share a book like this with quite a young baby.

Looking at books together can greatly develop vocabulary and understanding of the world, especially once a child realises that pictures are actually representations of real things. You can begin to teach colours, counting, shapes and other important concepts very gradually through the use of books. Many parents feel that they need to 'read a story' but this is not particularly helpful early on because the child will not follow the plot and remember from page to page. A young child wants to focus on one thing at a time; there may be a picture of a house she keeps coming back to, so talk about it! 'Look at the red roof . . . Count the windows . . . Is there a mummy inside? . . . There's a tree outside the house . . . ' All those little but vitally important words like 'on', 'next', 'under', can be easily introduced in a way that the child can recognise their meaning and learn to use them herself.

Looking at books and talking about them will boost children's language development. A small child learns much of his early language through everyday experiences. First words are likely to be names like 'Mummy', 'drink', 'biscuit', 'bath', 'teddy', 'dog' – things he meets all the time through touch, taste, sight, sound and feel. The limitless world of pictures and stories will open up new horizons and you will be amazed at how much your child can absorb and understand. Given the right encouragement, once toddlers begin to talk, their vocabulary will grow rapidly. Some words will be so cute they will go down into family tradition! Hedgehogs may become 'hug-hugs', elephants 'everknits' and hippos 'hibbambobboms'! Write them down because you will forget all the funny things your young children say and do and one day wish you could remember!

Make the local library a regular port of call so you can enjoy lots of books before you invest in those which become real favourites. Ask if there is a weekly story-telling session for under-fives. Always check out charity shops and jumble sales, as buying new books is very costly! Make sure you provide a variety of subject matter, sizes and styles.

There is much to be said for setting aside a short period each day for your toddler to look at his books, perhaps after lunch while you do a damage limitation exercise clearing up after the fish fingers and spaghetti hoops. Sit him comfortably somewhere companionably near to you, with enough light, and present him with a pile of books to wade through with a piece of apple to eat. Tell him that if he sits nicely you will come and read one with him in a while. With a full tummy he may be content to stay still and oblige. Of course, the traditional time for stories and books is bedtime, but your energy level and routine and the tiredness of the child may make you decide to do it during the day instead. Try story or song cassettes to soothe him off to sleep.

Always have a book for each child wherever you go, whether it is to the doctor's surgery, a ride on the tube or a visit to an elderly aunt. It will help them sit through the boring bits!

It is sad that so much of children's time is swallowed up by television viewing, replacing reading and other activities with the passive watching of sometimes worthless material. Make the effort with books and it will pay off! And when it is time for your child to learn to read she will be half-way there because she already understands what books are for; having always had them, she knows them to be interesting and fun.

THE GREAT OUTDOORS

It was February, the day was miserable and it looked suspiciously like rain. But Denise was getting her show on the road. Wellies, all-in-one suits, buggy hood and brolly were going on and up, a bag of duck crusts and a flask of hot tea was in her bag, and off they went – a bracing walk in the park with her two small sons. They were a hundred yards down the road when the black cloud overhead burst, soaking them and their enthusiasm for fresh air and exercise. 'Was it for this that I completed four years of university education?' Denise asked herself. But she jollied them along and determined not to admit defeat. Her subject had, after all, been philosophy – she'd done the theory, this was the practice!

There comes a time in many homes with pre-school children – often at about two or three o'clock in the afternoon – when the mother realises they will all be lucky to make it to bedtime without serious injury to her mental health, not to mention the happiness of her children. Often the best thing to do is to go out somewhere and for many of us with small children it becomes part of every day's routine. As well as being a break from being inside, a walk to the park and a play in the playground lets off some energy and may make them tired, although beware the tendency they may have to drop off to sleep on the way home just when you want to keep them awake!

You may be fortunate and have a garden. If you are able to invest in a strong climbing frame you will gain from it for years to come. Once you have taught your intrepid toddler how to climb safely, you can relax a little. A garden may mean you don't have to go out every day. Make quite sure there are no hazards in it. Is it properly fenced in? Could anyone get in and harm your child? Are there any poisonous plants, like laburnum pods or brightly coloured berries? Beware of ponds, dangerous places to climb, unstable bits of wood or stones piled up anywhere. Check carefully before letting children roam around – rather than after a visit to Accident and Emergency!

Bikes, sandpits, water-trays – the fun you can provide goes on and on. You might even allow the children a corner to dig and practice horticulture for themselves. In the summer, mix some paint, stick newspaper to the fence, give them a brush and let them at it! You can plan a variety of activities for the week. Your local swimming pool, the library, a visit to friends ... but you will probably have to come to terms with the need to do something child-oriented every afternoon. Even a trip round the supermarket might do, if you're really feeling up to it!

SURVIVING SHOPPING

A man was pushing a trolley round a supermarket. He was reaching the end of his shopping list and the baby with him was reaching the end of his tether! An elderly lady watched with interest – the child screaming, the father trying to restrain him from escaping from the trolley seat and speaking softly as he neared the checkout queue. 'It's OK, George, keep calm, George, we'll be home soon, George! George, don't panic now, hang in there, George ...' Approaching the father she remarked how impressed she was with his patience with the baby. The man looked puzzled. 'I mean the way you are trying to pacify little George,' the woman explained. 'Madam,' replied the man grimly, '*I'm* George!'

Those of us who routinely do the weekly big shopping trip with the assistance of a toddler know how blissful it is to go alone! But with a little forethought even the trip to the supermarket can provide reasonable entertainment without you ending up as distraught as George.

* Try to go when the children are fed, fairly good-tempered and not overtired.
* With smaller ones always take the kind of straps you use in a high chair or pram to secure them into the trolley-seat.
* Do your best to have a cheerful attitude even if it is your least favourite job. Supermarkets are colourful, interesting places in children's eyes.
* Go as quickly as possible through the beginning as by the end time will be against you. It is easier if you miss out the most tempting aisles – buy chocolate another time!
* When spirits begin to flag, produce a drink. A bit later a snack to keep them further occupied.
* Do not allow small children to bully you into buying things. Give them a few choices of two favourite cereals

or types of biscuit. If you ever once weaken your control you will be badgered every time you come. Demands of 'Mum, can we have some sweets?' you can do without!

ADVENTURES AT HOME

Toddlers thrive in the company of other children. Whether it's having a friend in to play or the experience of live-in entertainment in the shape of brothers and sisters, as your child grows older and more aware of other people he will enjoy the fun, chaos and even the inevitable conflict – provided you are around and ready to intervene when necessary!

This chapter began with mess and this is the word which will accurately describe any home with small children in it at about two o'clock, any afternoon. Unsupervised, a couple of toddlers can wreck a room in moments. With no thought beyond the actual moment they will pull out boxes of toys, empty cupboards, and squirrel away a cocktail mix of wooden bricks, dressing-up clothes, banana skins and lumps of play-dough under their beds or behind the sofa.

This drives many parents crazy. Although you may prefer to monitor and guide what goes on most of the time, now and again, if you are feeling unusually saintly, let them play dens. Even if you regret it afterwards, when the immediate area looks like the site of a major explosion, it is still worth it for the fun.

Otherwise, bring down a specific box of toys and concentrate on them. When whatever is in the box palls, tidy it away and fetch another. Even doing this occasionally will help, and you can make sure that less popular items are given an airing along with the daily favourites.

Generally speaking, children enjoy being around the house, joining in with whatever you are doing. But keep a watchful eye: who knows what may be going on!

With still two weeks of holiday left after a long rather inclement summer, each day found Val steadfastly trying to impersonate Supermum. 'I am going to feed the fish,' nine-year-old Julia informed her mother responsibly one morning. Sam, aged two-and-a-half, decided this sounded interesting and puffed up the stairs with his big sister. Now, up until this morning Val had successfully concealed from her toddler the whereabouts of Warsaw, a homeless goldfish once left by Polish neighbours off on holiday and never reclaimed. A real Supermum would have realised what would happen next, but this one was too busy in the kitchen to notice. *Crash, scream, shouts of horror and consternation.* Val sprinted upstairs to the spare room where Warsaw lived in his bowl on the tallboy to find Julia juggling with a breathless flapping goldfish. The carpet was sodden and sprinkled with pieces of gravel and water weed. The bowl was upside down, and Sam, drenched from head to toe, sat seriously traumatised and hopping mad. Val wiped the weed off her son's face, put dry clothes on him and gave him a cuddle. Apart from the shock, he was very cross because the sensation of sitting down suddenly on one of the stones felt to him as if the fish had bitten his bottom. It was his main topic of conversation for days. The fish was fine; he too survived to tell the tale.

SAFETY FIRST

Every family needs rules. Concern for the safety and welfare of our children will make us insist on some basics.

1. *Roads*. Golden rule: 'Never cross a road without holding someone's hand.' If you make this a law never to be broken, much of the danger from traffic will be eliminated. Talk about road safety from the time your baby can understand you. The constant repetition of warnings and comments about passers-by or vehicles going along will focus her attention on this issue and make it easier to teach the

basics later on. So comments like: 'Look at that red car, it's going fast and we must wait for it to go past.' 'That sensible girl is crossing by the green man.' 'Let's look and see if it's safe to cross', will all help.

2. *Parks and playgrounds.* Never take your eyes off a child in your care when you are in a public place. You can never tell if someone may be lurking who could frighten them or worse. Teach your child to use play equipment safely. Show him how to place his hands and feet on the climbing frame, how to position himself at the top of a slide ready to slither down. Watch for swings that can hit him and remind him to give them a wide berth. It is important to encourage small children to explore and develop their physical skills and in our anxiety for their safety not to make them so nervous that we quench their sense of adventure. There are some children who would benefit from their sense of adventure being quenched! But all the same, try to combine vigilance and caution with a relaxed approach.

3. *Shopping.* Always be vigilant. Never leave a baby or toddler outside a shop in a pram or pushchair and make sure they are strapped in at all times. Try not to take little ones on big shopping expeditions; their company will not bless you and it is all too easy for a bored toddler to wander off through the clothes racks and cause you heart palpitations until he is found again. He may even damage goods and get you both into trouble.

Jane was shopping in a small supermarket when she stopped to chat to a friend. Meanwhile her small daughter discovered the shelves of confectionery. It was only as they reached the checkout that Jane woke up to the fact that Tamsin had munched her way through most of a 500g pack of milk chocolate.

PEOPLE TO TRUST

We live in a dark world, and as parents we will seek to protect our children, alerting them to possible dangers but at the same time fostering the openness and trust which comes so naturally and enables them to make good relationships with other children and adults. It is a tragic reflection on our society that today we need to teach our children not to be too trusting of others. The sad truth is that many perpetrators of abuse are family members or others well known to the child.

* Be very careful to check on anyone who looks after your children.
* Teach your children to respond politely to strangers but not to enter into detailed conversation. Explain to them how to take their leave – 'I am going to find my mummy now, goodbye,' – and insist they never accept anything without their adult's permission. They must never go with anyone they don't really know. Teach them to find a shop assistant or someone else in a uniform if they lose you. Hopefully such precautions will never be needed but it is so much better to prepare them just in case. At as young an age as possible, your child should be able to recite his name, address and perhaps your phone number.

HEARTS AND MINDS

Children also need protecting from more subtle dangers too. So open and impressionable, they can be deeply – although often invisibly – affected by what they see or hear.

William woke at nine one evening and strayed into a room where adults were watching a harrowing TV news report about a conflict in an African country showing the mutilated bodies of murdered children in the battle zone. He stood unnoticed in the doorway, and tried to get his four-year-old brain round the terrifying images on the screen. His parents only realised he was there as he ran sobbing from the room.

Entertaining Toddlers

Unfortunate incidents like this can happen, but how can we be sure that the programmes our children watch in the daytime or early evening are not affecting them adversely? Do your best to be with your toddler and share the experience of TV with them – are there some jobs you could do at the same time? Whenever possible opt for a video which you know is harmless. Monitor what your children watch and take time to find out how much they understand. If you are unhappy about the content and quality of a programme turn it off and offer an alternative idea for their entertainment. There is so much that is excellent but regrettably some material that clearly is not, so be wise and firm in your judgment. Crass cartoons featuring rudeness, senseless violence and loud noise will not benefit young children. Too much watching makes them grumpy, unmotivated and addicted and also means they miss out on other creative and wholesome activities. Out of the twelve hours they are awake, how much time should be spent in front of the screen? What should they watch? How will you enforce your decisions?

There we have just one more of the host of dilemmas and decisions facing us every day as parents. We can only give it our best shot and see what happens.

9
GROWING UP

> Suddenly he wasn't a baby any more. The funny things
> he used to say and do were discarded now, along with
> the rattle he'd chewed to bits and the scratched old high
> chair. I saw he was ready for it – the beginnings of real
> independence. But was I?
>
> *A mother's reflections on her son's third birthday*

Once out of babyhood, young children start learning to live
life for themselves – albeit under the beady eye of a
constantly vigilant adult! The frustrated cry of '*Let me!!!*
I want to do it!' will try your patience for many a year to
come, but developing responsibility and independence is
what growing up is all about.

KEEPING CLEAN AND TIDY

Mary loves brushing her teeth. Unsupervised, she can
pulverise a tube of toothpaste in seconds, leaving white
streaks all down her front, in her hair and ears to prove it!
Washing is fun too – lots of soap trickling everywhere,
soggy sleeves and wet patches on the bathroom carpet.
Keeping small children clean, tidy and fed is a messy and
demanding business.

Practice makes perfect. If your child takes pleasure in
washing and sploshing water everywhere, let her do it.
This is easy in the summer; stripped and in the garden or
on the balcony, a washing-up bowl and 'clothes' or 'dishes'

to clean will keep her happy and help her learn about wetness! Think of a bath as a playtime as well as a pre-bed calmer and the necessary means of washing away the day's grime. Put a grumpy child in some warm bubbly water with plastic cups, jugs and funnels and preferably someone to join in, and she will probably cheer up. But remember never to leave the room if your children are under three – they can drown in a few inches of water. Even with three-and four-year-olds, check constantly and stay well in earshot.

Getting dressed. The sooner your toddler can put on a few of his own clothes, the sooner you won't have to! Choose easy garments: tracksuit bottoms and sweatshirts which are comfortable, practical and need no ironing! Begin with undressing – pulling off is easier – and use any tactic you can think of to motivate him: races, games, songs, stories ('I'll tell you the next part when your sock is off'). The simplest garments to put on are probably pants, so start with them. Dressing is an important skill and it is worth investing time teaching them how to do it themselves.

Meal times. In the early months of eating solid food, a baby has to be fed by someone else. You can become quite adept at shovelling mashed potato into an infant at the same time as your own lunch into you! Like an expert brick-layer, any extra food on his face can be gently scraped off and popped in the ever-opening mouth. It is time-consuming, and a relief when he begins to feed himself. However, the mess involved in letting a baby loose with his spoon and a bowl of rice pudding defies description! There are no short cuts to achieve presentable eating habits, it's just a phase with which you will just need to grin and bear.

FROM COT TO BED

Cots are really useful. When everything becomes too much, the doorbell rings, the soup boils over, you are desperate to visit the loo and your baby is howling – all at once – you can always put her in her cot and know that she is secure for two minutes while you attend to everything else. It is a comfort to know that there is a place where she is safe, especially at night when you are asleep. Be warned, though; one day she will master the cot bars and escape!

Once she has grown big enough to climb out, there is little point in continuing to use a cot. In fact it could now be a dangerous place for her to fall from.

Make as much mileage as possible from the new stage of sleeping in a 'big bed' – especially if you have a younger baby who will be needing to inherit the cot fairly soon. Be sure she is in no danger of a nasty fall from a big bed. Side rails are available or you could always create a soft landing. 'New' – albeit hand-me-down – bed linen or night clothes will add to the occasion and make her feel proud to be so grown up. Make it quite clear that once in bed she must not get out until called, and if you are concerned that she might still roam around the house, secure the door so it is ajar but not open enough to squeeze through.

OUT OF NAPPIES

Before your child starts a pre-school activity, around the age of about two, you will begin to train her to use the toilet. Many parents experience a sense of foreboding about this. Perhaps they feel under pressure because every other child seems to have abandoned nappies long before their own offspring shows the remotest interest in the world of potties and trainer pants! After going through it three times, my best advice is to relax about the whole issue. It is pointless to begin until the child's physical and emotional development means he is ready. Boys are often less easy to train than girls. There are thousands of theories, methods, opinions and stories to be heard.

Try to be unstressed about it all. You will need to be firm – but beware of making toilet training into a discipline issue and a battle of wills (or won'ts!). Talk to the child about how pleased he will be when he is old enough to leave off his nappy and explain that you are going to help him reach this goal. Take him to buy some attractive underwear and get them out of the drawer now and then to remind him that soon he will be able to wear them. The whole process could take less than a week or six months depending on when you start and how things go. Choose carefully when to begin – when there are others around to help (dads can be brilliant at this), perhaps during the summer when life is not too busy and the odd puddle in the garden is neither here nor there.

Decide what to do when you are going to be away from the potty for more than half an hour. Put a nappy on? Keep off drinks, drain his system before you leave and hope for the best? You may resign yourself to an accident and put him in trainer pants with some spares stuffed in your pocket. Whenever possible, take the potty with you!

Before you begin, knowing your toddler as you do, *think about some ground rules*. Never be angry about accidents – although if they persist because of laziness or plain naughtiness try introducing an incentive to encourage him, and be firm about what you want. If you are asking a child to do something well within his capability (like sitting on a potty or pulling down his pants) and he refuses, you can respond as you normally do to his not doing as he is told. Half the task is over if you can persuade him to sit happily on the potty for a few minutes with a book, a little drink perhaps and even a biscuit by way of encouragement; nature is then likely to take its course! If and when the brain communicates with the bowel or the bladder and the required deed is done – well, celebrate! Congratulations, praise and cheers are sure to encourage him to do it all again thirty minutes later!

Although Geoff and Sharon had gone through all this with their two older children, it was six years earlier. When it came to helping Holly with using a loo their memories were rather vague. But they made a record of what happened and their experience might help you.

Christmas 1991. Bought potty and introduced it with great enthusiasm to our two-year-old. She adored it, put it on her head, stood in it, stored bricks in it but looked completely incredulous when we told her what it was for. Even with alarmingly lifelike enactments by various members of the family, teddies and a favourite doll, Holly was not interested.

January to March 1992. Potty took up residence next to the bath. Round about the end of February, she accidentally sat on it just as she was getting in the bath and then produced an egg-cupful of urine.

Congratulations and celebrations. From then on Holly adopted the potty as a bath toy and would sometimes sit on it in the water and allegedly wee into it!

March to July 1992. Life was far too hectic for the family to devote any time to the potty project. Meanwhile, two of Holly's best friends mastered the whole thing and when they came to play we tried our best to enthusiastically commend their efforts without sounding condemning of our child's reluctance. She joined in with the encouragement but flatly refused to perform herself. We tried everything; using the loo (with or without a special seat), a blue potty, a yellow potty with a duck on it, in the morning, after meals, before a bath ... She would gladly sit, make a few wincing expressions on her face and then give up! But we noticed that now she would disappear into a discreet corner to fill her nappy in private. We reassured ourselves that time was on our side!

August 1992. The month of August seemed a good time for some intensive training. We had a couple of weeks at home and Jane and Alex were not at school. Day One. We assembled as a team and got briefed!

'Right, everyone, our project for the next few days (optimistic!) is to get Holly out of nappies and we're going to work together!'

Removed Holly's Pamper and invited her to sit on the potty.

'Don't want to. Want my nappy.'

'You sit on it and I'll read you your "Spot" book.'

'No potty, story on your lap.'

'Come on, be a big girl. Sit on the potty.'

'I don't like it!' (getting tearful).

Enter Daddy with a much more practical approach: 'Would you like a white chocolate button?'

'Yes!'

'When you've done a wee in your potty, you can have a button.'

'No potty.'

'No button then.'

We dropped the subject and five minutes later there was a puddle to mop up off the kitchen floor!

'No wee on the floor, wee in your potty.'

'*No!*'

It was at this point that they remembered the ruse of giving the child some irresistibly beautiful underwear. Geoff and Jane were at once sent off to buy some. They came back with some pretty amazing pink frilly knickers with teddies and balloons embroidered on the front. Six pairs! Holly fell in love with them and became so attached to them she refused to take them off – even when that evening she sat on the potty and did as she should!

Days Two to Four.   The soggy laundry was piling up. Day Five.   Quite suddenly Holly decided to co-operate and became super-efficient at potty-craft. Each time we reminded her, she would haul down her beloved pink pants and produce a sample. A difficulty came when we had to go out in the car to a friend's house, but when we arrived she quite happily used her potty in this different environment.

Day Seven.   Today we introduced her to some trainer pants. Now she has got used to wearing no nappy in the daytime, with the feeling of cotton knickers instead of the comforting tightness of a nappy, she was ready to try these plastic covered towelling 'heavy duty' jobs. No problem. They'll be useful for longer car journeys and later on, at night.

Mission accomplished!! Aged two years, eight months and one day!

It is surprising what a difference it makes to see your son or daughter out of nappies. It helps the housekeeping budget too! Babyhood is fading into the past. Soon you will be able to go on holiday without a pushchair, feeding cup, clip-on seat, and whatever other paraphenalia your child seems to need!

ALLOWING FREEDOM – WITH VIGILANCE

There are some nightmares which haunt every parent. The child who rushes after his ball into the busy street ... the baby who chokes in her cot, unattended in the dead of night ... the tiny lifeless body floating in the swimming pool ... even the threat of abduction or attack ... these are all images we hate to dwell on but hopefully result in our being extra vigilant over the children in our care. It would be easy to become near-paranoid over the dangers in childhood; we must find the right balance so that they can enjoy maximum freedom and independence but be safely protected. Accidents will happen, inevitably, but if they do, avoid the awful guilt you could feel because you ignored sensible precautions and practical ground rules.

RISKS AT HOME

The kitchen

The most hazardous part of most homes is the kitchen. Don't ever leave a mobile person under the age of four (if he's sensible by then) alone in the kitchen. It is a dangerous place as well as being the heart of family life.

The cooker. Teach your child early the words 'hot' and 'burn' with the help of a bit of dramatic explanation. Speak very sharply to him if he experiments with touching things he knows to be hot and consider a smack as a response if he persists in opening the oven door (even when it is off) or does some other risky action. It is worth buying a guard for the hob of your cooker to keep pans contained and fingers from knobs or flames. Always turn pan handles inwards to avoid terrible accidents by an inquisitive hand reaching up to a boiling pot on the stove.

Knives need to be stored out of reach (a magnetic strip on the wall is good, or in an inaccessible drawer) and also watched carefully while in use. Again, a graphic description of the dangers of cutting implements – scissors too – and an immediate outraged response at any messing about with these forbidden objects should mean the child understands. Don't forget other sharp things such as skewers, food processor blades, and table forks and knives.

Chemicals. Most of us find the most convenient place to keep bleach, dishwashing powder, cleaning creams and liquids and other deadly concoctions is in the cupboard under the sink. Unfortunately this is also a favourite place for many toddlers, mobile but still unreasonable at twelve months, curious and mischievous at eighteen months and accident-prone, fascinated and downright naughty at two years! If this is the case for you, swap the cleaning fluids over with a collection of pans, plastic bowls, sieves, funnels and other harmless clutter so your child can play safely. If he does drink a poisonous substance, read the directions on the bottle for an antidote and dial 999 fast.

Many parents fit safety catches on fridges, cupboard doors and drawers to keep toddlers out. You may find these almost impossible to manipulate yourself when you need to open something, whereas your streetwise toddler manages them with his eyes shut.

Stairs

A *stair-gate* is a useful investment – although you may find you need many of them to adequately block off every flight of stairs or out-of-bounds room. It is wise to teach children to manage stairs and help them to climb up and down them safely as early as possible. In the daytime, put sofa cushions at the bottom in case of a fall.

Bathrooms

Baths are a good stand-by when nothing else seems to entertain your children and they need a bit of relaxation. A capful of bubbles, some toys and even a sibling to join them (if you can cope with the sopping wet floor afterwards!) keeps a toddler happy while you finish something off or just have a quick breather before the tea-time stint begins! *No young child should be left in a bath unwatched*.

The medicine cabinet, often sited in the bathroom, should be locked and well out of reach. *Cleaning fluids*, especially toilet cleaners, must also be hidden away.

The toilet itself is obviously a hazardous place where germs breed and loo rolls become mysteriously waterlogged! As your toddler learns to use the lavatory on his own, make sure no mischief is being committed up there!

Other hazards

Take care with *electrical appliances*, plugs and sockets. Use plastic covers to protect curious children from the consequences of poking things into interesting holes in the wall. Ensure your child's bedside light can do him no harm if he fiddles with it.

Never leave *dangerous machines* (lawnmowers, hedge cutters and drills in the garden, knives, food processors and fat friers inside) where small children can get at them.

STARTING PLAYGROUP

Jennie was on her way to attend playgroup for the first time. At nearly three, she was outgoing and well used to being left in a variety of creches. She and her mum had popped in to visit the playgroup a few times before and Sara was confident that Jennie would settle happily but it was very important to get this first morning right. This is how it went:

Sara had already explained to her daughter that she was going to stay at playgroup without Mummy. Now she repeated this, telling Jennie she was leaving in a minute to get lunch ready and would come back when it was ready. She took the child on her lap and talked about all they could see in the room. Looking around through Jennie's eyes, the prospect looked pretty hazardous – any self-respecting toddler would hang on to her mum at the sight of all those enormous four-year-olds hurtling past on police bikes, dogs on wheels and beaten up Postman Pat vans.

After a while Jennie was busy with some play-dough and Sara gradually distanced herself physically. By the door she called 'Good-bye!', gave a final wave, blew a last kiss and went. Jennie hardly noticed and had a wonderful morning with her new friends.

In the weeks that followed, occasionally something would unsettle her and she'd cling and cry when it was time to say goodbye. Sara would stay a little longer, trying to interest Jennie in a favourite activity and then firmly insist on leaving – even if it meant leaving her child in tears, which always disappeared seconds after her mother had gone.

This may not be your experience. When the time comes to start some kind of pre-school activity there may be anxiety and misery for both parent and child.

Hannah was an only child. Brought up in difficult circumstances by her single mother, she was quite withdrawn and nervous. Gloria had done her very best in her parenting – she was devoted to her daughter, and up until now she'd never consented to leaving the child with anyone else unless she was fast asleep. Hannah had had everything her mother could give and do for her but when it was time to start at nursery school she was far from prepared. Leaving Hannah was impossible; she screamed hysterically and Gloria could not bear leaving her. It took nearly a month to settle her.

LETTING GO

It is so important to know when and how to let them go. It applies to everything – like that heart-stopping experience of watching him climb a high slide for the first time, wobble as he negotiates the top of the ladder, change to a sitting position and then triumphantly slide down. You are thinking all the time that the steps are too far apart, the guard rails too flimsy and the sides too low, but this step of independence – provided you are sure he is capable of it – has to come and you must grit your teeth and cheer him on enthusiastically!

Teach him to be careful but don't be so anxious you make him nervous and unadventurous himself! It is not easy to balance being protective with encouraging his independence. But, he's growing up – fast – and it's time to start letting go.

PART THREE
REAL-LIFE ISSUES

10

PLAYING AND LEARNING

I see and I forget.
I hear and I remember.
I do and I understand

Chinese Proverb

There's so much more to learning than just being taught. In the course of our lives we have to grasp millions of things, facts and figures, skills like walking and talking, the ability to relate to others and come to terms with our own feelings and hopes. Our Chinese proverb hints at how this is best done.

In his early teens Jamie learned how to sail a dinghy. A born bookworm he first spent hours reading it all up, and memorised the special names for all the bits of the boat, understood the ways to set the sails, found out how to go against the direction of the wind and read what to do in an emergency. Confidently, he climbed into that little 'Heron' class boat for the first time – but much to his consternation found there was more to sailing than simply following instructions in a book. Everything kept flapping, the boat would not stay on an even keel and sometimes when Jamie tried to steer in a certain direction, nothing happened at all!

Fortunately, his older brother was a patient teacher and was on hand to help him apply what he'd read in the manual to real life. In no time at all Jamie had grasped the basics: hanging over the side holding on by his toes as the two boys sailed into the wind, half tipping into the water; controlling the small jib-sail so as to catch as much wind in it as possible; getting the feel of the tiller in his hand as he steered through the water, and even getting the boat upright again when a sudden gust of wind capsized her.

LEARNING FOR LIFE

Those skills, now learned, will stay with Jamie for ever. Perhaps you can ride a bike, handle a horse or drive a car. When you learned how to do these things you may not have consulted a manual but relied mainly on the person who was teaching you, and on 'hands-on' experience. You found out through your successes and failures, by hard work and practice.

It's just the same for small children. They learn best from the right combination of understanding, experience, encouragement, help from others and lots and lots of repetition!

Babies are born with basic instincts, huge potential but no knowledge, skills or ideas. It's great fun as a parent – and an awesome responsibility at times – to be involved in the child's process of learning. Newborns possess certain abilities – how to cry and suck for instance – and each individual is uniquely gifted genetically with innate talents and potential to develop as they grow. There are those who from an impossibly early age display amazing musical, mathematical or artistic skills. There is something special in each human being and as parents we have the privilege of overseeing, guarding and guiding developing skills, character and understanding.

. HOW IT BEGINS

From the first hours of life, provided all is well and in good working order, our children experience sounds, movement, light and darkness and physical feelings through their senses. After birth, some things keep happening – the smell of warm milk and the feeling and taste of drinking it, the comfort of being held and cuddled, the sound of parents' voices or the sensation of being pushed in a pram. As she begins to recognise these repetitive experiences, your baby starts the lifelong adventure of making sense of her world. Soon, she will expect the taste of milk to follow its sweet smell and a particular way she is being held. She'll anticipate the sight of her smiling dad just after the sound of his footsteps and her siblings' excited voices welcoming him home again.

Babies are programmed to learn, but their development can be slowed down if they are cut off from life.

A young Indian couple lived on the ninth floor of a tower block. Rezer was out at work from eight in the morning until ten o'clock at night, leaving Sita and their baby, Tariq, at home. Sita spoke little English and had no friends or family nearby, so she was very nervous about leaving her flat. She spent almost all her time alone and became very withdrawn and depressed. The home was spotlessly clean and the baby well cared for – but Sita didn't realise that Tariq needed more than this to grow and develop. She never talked or played with him, showing him and letting him feel, taste or listen to new things. Rezer, when he came home, was too tired and he didn't know much about babies either. Only when another Asian family who understood the couple's culture and their situation came to live next door did things get better. They showed Rezer and Sita how to stimulate and bring on their baby and with their support and help three-month-old Tariq quickly caught up.

BABIES AT PLAY

In a surprisingly short time, babies start learning all manner of things. In the first year they grasp the mechanics of using their bodies, the basics of communication, the art of interpreting the happenings around them and the fascinating law of cause and effect!

Babies all go through a stage when their main pleasure in life seems to be watching the objects they drop fall to the ground. This is followed by inconsolable wails until someone retrieves whatever it is for the eager student of physics to repeat the experiment all over again. Believe it or not, this is education!

What is she learning?

Well, first she's finding out about the object itself; that it is smooth or bumpy, hard or squeezy, bright and interesting or plain. Then, she has to try and get her fingers round to grasp it. She waves her hand and sees that the object waves with it, stuck to her hand. Next she puts her hand over the edge of the pram, cot or high chair and waves it in mid-air. Three minutes elapse before the next possibility dawns; the fist unwraps itself and 'hey presto!', *clonk*! out of sight, on to the floor. Gone. Forever. She shouts and at this point Daddy walks over to her, lovingly wipes her dribbly chin, has a little chat and smilingly, like the miracle man she is increasingly realising he is, gives her back the dropped toy. She holds it and chuckles. Life is so full of fun! She does the whole thing over and over again and learns that exactly the same things happen each time – except that the smile on Daddy's face is wearing a bit thin by the fifth occasion. Young Lisa is learning – all sorts of things – and so is Dad!

MASTERING BASIC SKILLS

Young children have to master a large number of physical skills. Everything from holding spoons to climbing ladders, controlling their bladders and bowels, to balancing, hopping and jumping, needs to be learned. Many of these accomplishments are arrived at naturally and easily but some physical skills are harder to achieve. Life can be very puzzling sometimes. Understanding adults who can patiently encourage and help make all the difference to a child's attitude and progress in learning.

Elaine remembers vividly when her children were toddlers and determined to feed themselves. She observed one day the unbelievable mess one of them was creating from a pot of banana yoghurt. Pretending she wasn't looking, Elaine watched her husband supervising the situation; he was obviously longing to take the spoon and do it for the child but knew it was much more important for her to learn to master this difficult operation herself. Patience and a good wash afterwards was all she needed and six months later she was eating like a princess – well, more or less!

PLAYING SAFE

We may sometimes over-restrict our infants because we are too afraid they will get hurt. Part of being a parent is experiencing that awful heart-stopping feeling when your toddler launches himself unaided for the first few times on a climbing frame, slide, or other playground equipment! Of course we must be constantly alert for danger, never allowing small children out of sight unless they are undoubtedly safe, but at the same time let us not be overprotective. A child will only learn to climb safely, judging footholds and distances, when he's discovered how easy it is to fall. Bruised knees quickly heal and the lessons they teach are worth a library of tree-climbing manuals!

Fathers are especially good at encouraging self-confidence and a sense of adventure; sometimes women are more aware of the possibilities of disaster! Lyndon spent hours with Daniel, Emma and Andrew, from babyhood on, encouraging and teaching them to try new feats and skills, whether in the swimming pool, the climbing frame or up a tree. The best game of all was for each to take turns at rushing along the path at breakneck speed to hurl themselves into his (thankfully) never-failing arms! Neither they nor their father needed any encouragement; but often parents may need to spend more time gently helping more timid children to conquer their fears and uncertainty.

LISTENING AND TALKING

As well as physical achievements, babies also need to learn to communicate and use their minds. Child psychologists tell us that children can only learn certain things at certain stages. We may draw our children on, introducing new activities and experiences that will stimulate the learning processes, but it is pointless to force a child before he is ready. We must wait until his fingers are agile and strong enough to grip a crayon before teaching him to draw. In his mental development too there comes the right moment for the next stage in his understanding.

When Paul was nine months old he was very fond of Golda, the family dog. He laughed and waved his arms at the labrador every time she went by and sometimes he managed to feel the soft fur and had a quick lick from her hot wet tongue when nobody was looking! He heard her name often; sometimes crossly, or loudly to call her to eat, and at other times with gentleness and affection. Paul cottoned on that this word 'Golda' had something to do with the gorgeous, furry, licky, funny creature that fascinated him so much. Round about the same time he noticed other word labels too: he had one, 'Paul', so did the place he went to sleep, 'cot', and the red thing with juice in it was 'drink'. After a few months he tried his first experiment. Pointing to the dog Paul shouted '*Dolda!*' and so much excitement and adulation was caused by this utterance, he was encouraged to go further and soon produced three more words; '*Daul!*', '*Dot!*' and '*Dink!*' for his admiring public!

As well as his mind working out the connection between words and objects, Paul also needed months of practice using his vocal cords, tongue and lips in the fun of making different noises. He needed to listen to others talking back to him and thrived on their encouragement as he tried out new sounds. He also had to realise the usefulness of speech for getting what he wanted. Once Paul got under way with talking there was no holding him! A small child – just like us – learns most effectively by experience.

EXPERIMENTS

How did Lisa learn all about water, sinking and floating? This is the same character who a year or so earlier drove her parents crazy dropping toys over the side of the pram. At two-and-a-half or three, if she could find a bucket full of water, or better still, the loo, she'd drop things in there too. Along with the inevitable discovery that water makes things (clothes, shoes, carpets ...) wet, she also saw that not everything falls to the bottom of the pail; some objects float. At this stage she didn't realise she had found anything out; it took repeat performances and some guidance from an adult who could give her some new words to describe what was happening and encourage her to think and talk about it. By four or five, Lisa could explain that stones go to the bottom but cork floats because the one is heavy and the other isn't. And when she was older still, she had to think again when she saw a heavily laden car ferry steam out of Folkestone Harbour ...

You may ask, 'But why does a three-year-old have to research sinking and floating in my nice dry house?' She needs to find out about the world she lives in wherever and however she encounters it, and to be equipped and encouraged – especially by adults sharing experiences, words and knowledge with her. It doesn't have to be messy; her experiments can happen in the bath, a patio or garden. A good playgroup will provide endless opportunities for this kind of discovery play too.

There is so much to discover. Young children need to learn about themselves, the people around them and the unseen mysterious awareness of spiritual life too. Children have an amazing ability to pick things up along the way and we can be their most effective teachers, often just by the power of example. If we can give them time and attention and let them enjoy all kinds of experiences we'll have the joy of seeing our babies and toddlers each developing their unique individual skills and abilities and growing into the people God made them to be.

THE RIGHT ENVIRONMENT

Starting from when your baby is very young, it is a good idea to make the effort to get out of the house or flat for some fresh air and a change of scenery. Sometimes your outing will just be a trip to the supermarket, post office or simply 'round the houses'. Other days, you'll go and see friends, visit your local park or go swimming.

As the children get bigger, there are lots of other ways to entertain them and there will soon be firm favourites of things to do and places to go.

1. In most areas of the country there are local fields, trees, parks or neighbourhood playgrounds. Even tiny babies enjoy a gentle swing sometimes, so long as they feel safe! As well as going on the equipment, what about feeding the ducks, visiting a favourite low climbing tree, watching the man mowing the grass or simply stopping to admire an attractive flower bed or a wild hedgerow. Anything can be made to be interesting and educational to young children with a bit of patience and enthusiasm!

2. Your local authority may provide special facilities for pre-school children. If you are not sure, contact the Under Fives Officer to find out what is available. There may be a One O'Clock Club where you and your child can paint, play, run about and generally make merry with other children and the playleader. Playgroups often welcome parents with toddlers at a small charge. Find out about your local swimming pool's special 'duckling sessions' for babies and under fives when it is not full of energetic school-age children making lots of splash and noise. Check out for Roly Poly Clubs where your toddler can bounce on an

inflatable instead of on you or your furniture. Join the local library. This was one of the first things I did after registering our children's births! It's never too soon to introduce books, and many children's libraries have a storytime slot once a week. And it's free! Are there any museums or mini-zoos, farms, duckponds, fields with donkeys, cows or sheep? All these will provide a hour or two's exercise, entertainment and opportunity for your children to learn as you talk to them about it.

3. Set time apart to sit on the floor and just play. Make a Duplo castle, a Stickle-brick monster or rearrange the dollies and cars. Sometimes direct what is going on to help your child gain more from her toys and at other times allow her to guide you. If you are the father, and out of the house for much of the child's waking week, this is a marvellous way of getting to know each other and giving your partner a break at the same time.

4. Maximise on the ordinary things you have to do. Play in the bath. Talk about whatever you're doing and that way you will teach the child new words and phrases. Let him watch you polish your shoes, and get dressed. Sit him safely up on the work top while you peel the vegetables and allow him to join in with jobs in the garden or unpacking the shopping. My mother always maintained, 'There is no job which is made easier by having a toddler (or even a five-year-old) helping!' She used to let us help all the same and never regretted the extra minutes it took. The brief years of childhood quickly pass – even if this week feels as if it is going on forever

5. Use stories, books, songs and rhymes along with whatever you're doing. Look at the world through your children's eyes and you can become nearly as excited about tractors and ducks and little purple flowers as they are. Lindsay was driving along one day keeping up her normal running commentary in a manner to rival the most highly qualified tour guide. Suddenly she realised there were no toddlers in the back of the car to listen

to her eulogising over the yellow tractor she had just passed. She realised she needed a holiday.

6. Allow them to make a mess as often as you can bear it! – to create dens, dress up or daub themselves with children's face make-up. In the summer, pin newspaper to the garden fence and let them loose with washable paints.

7. Maximise on the plans you have for each day. If you're going to the swings, take a picnic, even if it is only a bottle of squash and some apples. Take time to stop to say 'hello' to the donkey in the field on the way back from where you've been. Include surprises and fun wherever you can and try never to be in a hurry. Toddlers move like tortoises, particularly when they know you are short of time.

8. All this requires enormous energy, patience and motivation. Some days it's as much as you can do to survive until bedtime without laying on a three-ring circus as well. Know when to rein in, and be realistic at times of stress and strain. They'll survive and accept the situation. But otherwise we do well to remember these days will soon be gone. They may not feel priceless now, but I promise you'll look back with a smile at the memories.

11

LOVING OUR CHILDREN

If a child lives with criticism
He learns to condemn.
If a child lives with hostility
He learns to fight.
If a child lives with shame
He learns to feel guilty.
If a child lives with tolerance
He learns to be patient.
If a child lives with encouragement
He learns confidence.
If a child lives with praise
He learns to appreciate.
If a child lives with fairness
He learns justice.
If a child lives with security
He learns to have faith.
If a child lives with approval
He learns to like himself.
If a child lives with acceptance and friendship
He learns to find love in the world.

Dorothy Law Nolte

The most precious – and undoubtedly the costliest – gifts we
can give our sons and daughters are our time and our love.
Nothing is more important to human beings than to be
loved. This is a crucial need along with the basics for
physical survival, and those who never experience it will
limp through life, incomplete and never quite at rest.

The babe in your arms needs to grow up to know security, to be valued for the individual she is and to feel that her life has significance and purpose. Parents are key people in this process from the earliest age. So what does loving your child really entail? 'Love' is the most over-worked word in the English language and at the same time, the least understood!

INSTINCTIVE LOVE AND BONDING

There is a lot of talk about the importance of bonding with our babies. What is it? Dr Christopher Green writes:

> Bonding refers to that unique relationship which develops between parents and their child ... a special brand of love. I believe in bonding, but not in its elevation to a position of compulsive religion ... mums being told how they should feel by someone who thinks they know it all because they read some academic textbook. I also object to the view that there is a critical period of bonding, and if you mess it up in the early days, a lifetime of emotional hardship is guaranteed. Not true – if bonding doesn't happen at birth this does not mean it will never happen at all. It just needs patience and the right environment for Nature to take its course.

The process of bonding can come as rather a shock! Brigitte vividly recalls looking out at the view one misty autumn morning, resting her 'bump' on the window-sill of the baby's room and day-dreaming about the future. Suddenly, with no warning, a feeling of fierce, protective passion towards this unborn child came over her and she stood for several minutes weeping, amazed at how strongly she felt. Brigitte's story is not unusual. Caused by hormones, cultural influences, fears for the future, a natural instinct ... that strong parental love is very real for most parents.

I say most, because we are all different and so is the way we experience things. Sarah, now one of the most affectionate and loving mothers I know, felt absolutely nothing towards her baby during pregnancy and felt desperately guilty that she wasn't filled with maternal devotion until some days or weeks after his birth. And Penny, a quiet, rather shy mother, found her feelings matched her personality, a steady, undramatic but none the less powerful emotional tie to her baby.

That sense of longing and desire towards a child is sometimes strongest in the case of childless couples, who sadly have no baby of their own to love. In the years before our first pregnancy, after Lyndon and I were told that we were incapable of producing our own baby, I felt desperate, angry, frustrated – and bereaved. I longed to experience motherhood and it was a real fight to stop the desire for a child from becoming an obsession. Men and women in this position are often (but not always) suffering emotional turmoil and will be easily hurt by insensitive comments or personal questions.

FATHERS AND BABIES

Especially when it's their first child, some men may find it takes a while to fall in love with a new baby; those first weeks aren't easy at the best of times and nobody could have told you how radically life would change! Your wife feels sore, tired and almost taken over by this infant – leaving you to fend for yourself. Sleeping through the night is a pleasant memory of the past and the whole of your home seems to be dominated by this tiny person!

Mark thought the whole experience was like a nightmare. He felt helpless and upset as he watched the way Janie suffered the pain of labour, and guilty that it was because of him she'd become pregnant at all. The moment of birth was almost frightening – blood always made him feel faint – and when they finally handed the baby to him Mark felt emotionally wrung out. It took weeks before he fully recovered and could feel anything but a kind of anger towards their child. But as the memories faded so did these reactions, and it was not long before he was trying to persuade his wife to think about a baby brother or sister for little Charlie.

Some couples prefer the father not to be there when their babies are born – that's fine and nobody should feel they are 'second class' because of it.

Andy wanted to be present at the birth of his children – and quite apart from the strength and help that was to Dana, he says he would not have missed it for the world and believes that being there from the first moment set his relationship with each one off to a good start. However, he found his relationship and feelings really came alive as the children reached their first birthday.

Maybe as a dad, you're feeling slightly superfluous in these early days when the mother takes the main role in caring for the child. Because of this intense activity, women usually form a close relationship with the child quickly despite the mess, exhaustion and loss of freedom involved. But don't be discouraged, you can begin to build your own relationship with the baby too. Just holding your son or daughter – even when you're nervous about which end might do what! – and talking to him or her is a start. One grandfather always recommended cricket commentaries as a soothing way to keep babies happy; I daresay any sport would do! Love will dawn on you eventually even if it's not there from the start, a father-love just as strong as a mother's which will instinctively want to protect and provide for this person who is a part of you.

SPECIAL CHILDREN

1. Adoption. Mary and Luke could have no children of their own and decided to adopt. Almost three years later, after scores of interviews, investigations and frustrations, they were

accepted as prospective adoptive parents. 'It was a very difficult experience to go through,' they said. 'Only the hope of having a child kept us going.' One day, out of the blue, the phone call came and forty-eight hours later an eleven-month-old boy moved in with them, later adopted as their own son.

Obviously this couple had not bonded with Sam from birth nor he to them. The first weeks were not easy as the child missed the foster mother who had cared for him since birth. But gradually he responded to Luke and Mary more and more as they loved him and patiently waited for him to become attached.

2. Children with disabilities. We all, understandably, hope for healthy, normal children. In fact most parents expect this, so if they discover there is something wrong it comes as a shock.

The joy the Dawson family felt at the birth of Sarah was unbounded. She was perfect, and they could hardly wait to take her home. But when the paediatrician did the routine check he discovered all was not well: her horrified parents were warned that she could be deaf, blind and perhaps have learning difficulties too. 'It was as if she was someone else's baby, not our Sarah. I looked at her and dreaded the future. We felt numb, disappointed and empty.' The earlier bonding now seemed irrelevant; Sarah's parents had to fall in love with her again. It took time, tears and determination that they would give their daughter every ounce of their love and commitment in the difficult years to come.

GIVING LOVE

There is no relationship that will demand love quite like being a parent! From before they are born, we have a responsibility to care for our children; and we need a God-given, self-giving love to do so.

Both before, when pregnancy seems to go on for ever, and after the grand arrival, there are bound to be times of real resentment and frustration towards our howling,

111

hungry offspring, especially in the small hours of the morning! But it is crucial that your child knows he is loved. As Josh McDowell, an internationally known expert on teens, says, 'Your kid should know you're crazy about him.' Above and beyond all the inevitable mistakes, the negative things regrettably said or done, the anger and impatience that every parent goes through, they need to experience our committed unchanging love and know we're 'for them' – even at the times when we don't much *like* their behaviour!

Some parents find it isn't easy to love like this.

Maria was eighteen and more than anything else she wanted to have a baby, so she deliberately set out to become pregnant. Desperate to get away from her family, who were constantly at each other's throats, she longed for someone who was just hers to really love her. The reality was very different. Maria and her baby were moved into a seedy 'bed and breakfast' for the first six months, awaiting a council flat. Kylie suffered from colic and screamed all day and whatever Maria tried, it didn't work. In the end she felt so defeated, so cheated and so angry, she found herself copying the kind of things her dad had done to her when she was little. She shouted, shook and smacked her daughter in her frustration and loneliness at yet another person in her life who seemed just to use her and wouldn't love her.

This sad story, similar to those of other mothers coping on their own, has a happy ending. Maria got the support and help she desperately needed from some people in a local church and now she's doing much better, learning to live a more fulfilled life both as an individual person and a mother.

It was understandable for Maria to want her baby to love her. But being a parent means you have to learn how to love with the expectation that there may be nothing in return. As far as small children are concerned, you exist solely for their benefit, to provide food, drink, comfort, security – and entertainment. The average two-year-old is not likely to tell you how marvellous you are, massage your back or make you a cup of tea when you feel all in! If he thinks you are a bit preoccupied, he may throw a tantrum to demand even more of your attention!

One wet, cold afternoon, Meena was totally at the end of her tether with her two toddlers. They were all dressed for a trip to the park but, drained and exhausted, Meena subsided tearfully on to the bottom stair right in front of them. 'More than anything else I wanted a caring arm around my shoulder or a kiss, a word of encouragement and cheering smile – or even five minutes' break from the endless questions and calls for help!' What did she get? A fight broke out immediately. One child began to shout and stamp his feet while the other emptied the plastic bag of stale bread, meticulously cut into duck-size pieces, all over the carpet. They completely ignored their weeping mum because they could not begin to enter into how she was feeling and did not know how to help. 'Mummy! Park! Feed ducks!'

There wasn't much option really.

'Off we go, then,' sighed Meena, and they went.

To expect a baby or even a pre-school child to give you much emotional support is inappropriate. We need to draw on our own inner resources, family and adult friendships to provide that. Be content with your little one's deep and growing attachment to you, the total dependence and the beauty to be seen in a gummy, beaming grin! And year by year, as she grows up, she'll love you back.

SETTING AN EXAMPLE

By showing care and appreciation within your home and among close family and friends, children learn from you about real love. For parents who are not alone, one very important way to bring the security and knowledge of love to your little son or daughter is to express your affection and commitment to your partner. Potential forces of jealousy, rejection, aggression and many other negative things may be held at bay in a child who knows definitely that love – even though it is not perfect – lives in his house and is shared by everyone in it.

UNREAL EXPECTATIONS

Part of our feelings towards our children as infants will be bound up with how we think and hope they'll turn out. For years before Gareth and Sharon had any children, Sharon used to day-dream about how family life would be; conjuring up pictures in her mind of happy sunny days in the garden, walks by the sea and all the Christmases to come. When they were born, she and Gareth fell in love with each baby – but Sharon recognised she was also rather in love with the whole idea of having children and all that went along with it.

Don, a brand new dad, rushed out before the shops shut and bought a Hornby train-set for his three-hour-old son, and there is an eccentric couple who appear in the Guinness Book of Records for naming their firstborn after the entire team of the Liverpool Football Club. We all have dreams and there's nothing wrong with that – so long as we adapt our ideas of the ideal dream boy or girl as we get to know and come to terms with the real one we were sent!

There is also the danger that we can look to our children to achieve our own unfulfilled ambitions, hoping they'll succeed in the things we never did. Penny had to cut short her degree course because she was pregnant. During the next ten years she had a succession of babies and life was filled with the responsibility of motherhood. By the time she was a little more free she did not feel able to go back to her studying, but she found her highest ambition was for her four boys to do well at school. It was only when the youngest showed signs of emotional stress that she realised what an unfair pressure she put on her sons, trying to make them into people that perhaps they weren't. She wanted them to achieve her ambitions but they needed to grow and develop to be themselves.

It's right to have goals for our children, to encourage them and stretch them where necessary. But the slightly romanticised love that is hoping for an unreal future, needs to be watched and tempered.

PHYSICAL AFFECTION

The pleasure of holding, cuddling, kissing and playing with your baby is hard to match. Affectionate and demonstrative love is a vital component for his whole development. Research has shown that infants who are merely fed, changed and left in their cots for the first weeks fail to thrive as well as babies who are shown plenty of physical love.

Hold and stroke your child as she feeds. Speak to her gently, and always – however short you are of time – linger a few moments for a cuddle after you pick her up or before you put her back down to sleep. This will come easily for some parents but others may for one reason or another feel awkward or inhibited. Showing your children physical affection, from babyhood right through to adulthood, will serve to build security and self-esteem into their lives, help them come to terms with their own sexual identity – the masculine and feminine within themselves – and teach them to know how to relate physically to other people around them.

Geraldine had bad memories of her childhood. Rejected by her parents and never physically or emotionally loved when she was little, Geraldine was raped at the tender age of fourteen. She did get married later and was very happy, but when her son was born it took months of help and encouragement from both friends and professionals to help her to show him love freely in physical ways.

Whilst the taboo and deep-rooted fears of abuse need to be faced and talked out with a trusted counsellor or friend, it must be done in such a way that the seriousness and devastating effects of this problem are never minimised. Tremendous resources and expertise are needed to combat this evil lurking in so many lives in Britain today. Fortunately, help is available and should be sought by anyone who feels they need it.

As our babies grow into toddlers and then three- and four-year-olds, their delight and appetite for all kinds of affectionate behaviour from their parents seems to increase! The greatest joy in any four-year-old's life may be a 'tickle-fight' when she screeches for both mercy and more, all in the same breath as she and her father play rough and tumble on the floor. You will probably enjoy it as much as the child, although for those parents who are rather more reserved, remind yourself to pick her up frequently for a cuddle and tell her how wonderful you think she is.

Love. It is at the heart of all healthy relationships, and parents are the first examples and givers of it. Love must be constant, freely expressed ... and love must be tough! Sooner or later we will come face to face with the will-power of our children. Our attitude needs to be firm, unflappable, fair and full of love.

12
TRUE LOVE IS SOMETIMES TOUGH

Teach a child how he should live and he will remember
it all his life.

The Book of Proverbs

A key aim of parenting is to help our children to see, accept
and love themselves just for who they are. As we offer praise
and gentle correction we can help them begin to understand
their strengths and weaknesses. Children who are secure in
the love of their parents, who believe they matter as
individuals and are confident that their lives have significance, are more likely to respond to our efforts to help them
change areas of behaviour or character needing attention.

Discipline on its own does not work and can be harmful,
but a loving attitude, fair rules and consistent standards can
do much to affirm the good, discourage the bad and
beautify the ugly!

DISCIPLINE BEGINS WITH LOVE

1. Without it becoming a meaningless ritual, it is a good
check to ask ourselves each day if we've said '*I love you*', or
something similar to a child. Take time to stop, for no
apparent reason, take his hands in yours, smile into his eyes
and give him the gift of those words we all long to hear. Of
course, love needs to be demonstrated in action on a daily
basis to the child, but words have incredible power, so it

makes sense to make a habit of saying 'I love you!' – with sincerity.

2. *Be positive!* Take every opportunity to make approving comments and reinforce good behaviour. Even before a baby can understand simple phrases, positive language and tones of voice should be part and parcel of any interaction with him. A child who has a good picture of herself is more likely to behave well. Naughty children are sometimes that way because they feel bad about themselves and are trying to cover up their emotions, express their anger and disappointment or demand the attention of adults. No two people are the same; some of us are naturally more compliant, others seriously strong-willed from the start of life, and most are a mixture of both. The experiences of parenting probably teach us more about the basic waywardness of human nature – even in the smallest, best advantaged, most adorable person – than anything else.

3. *Build up your child.* Children can easily be discouraged. A child starting nursery school was asked what his name was. 'David Don't,' he replied. He had so often heard these words from his parents' lips they had become part of him.

As a parent, stick positive labels on too. Tell your child about her lovely qualities, not letting the things you love about her be completely eclipsed by the ghastly ones! Give simple compliments: 'You have a beautiful smile. It cheers me up.' 'I love the way you draw cars.' 'You are very kind and gentle with the kitten.' 'What a brilliant girl you are on the climbing frame!' Build in positive images, tell the truth and draw attention to her own good behaviour. Reward her, don't just be thankful that this time she didn't behave badly and say nothing. Everyone thrives on encouragement and appreciation. Toddlers and pre-school-age children are no exception.

The average toddler needs to be told 'No!' or 'Don't' several times each day and so there is a pressing need also to communicate lots of 'Yes!'s and 'Well done!'s. Particularly if you have a strong-willed child who seems bent on straining your patience to the utmost, a strategy needs to be worked out to take as many opportunities as possible to praise verbally, encourage and demonstrate approval and pride in what she is doing. See it as a challenge to tell her twice as many positives as negatives.

Watch out for the compliant child. Oddly enough, a toddler who causes little or no trouble may lose out on positive remarks because you thankfully take her good behaviour for granted. Comments like 'You did that really well', 'Well done', 'I am very pleased with you', 'I love the way you did that' are invaluable but easily left unvoiced if sweetness and light appears to be the norm for her. Just because a child is 'good', it doesn't necessarily mean she feels secure, loved, confident and at peace. She needs as much positive encouragement as her 'naughty' sister.

Like a golden thread, love must run through every aspect of parenting and especially the issue of discipline. That first recognition that your child is not made of unmitigated goodness is a sad moment! Sooner or later sounds of rebellion – however muted – will be heard. It may be a screaming fit at not having his own way, spitting out food for fun or perhaps a refusal to settle down to sleep – and provided you are quite sure that the child is not suffering in any way or expressing a real fear, pain or discomfort, your response needs to be lovingly firm and unmistakable. This is maybe the hardest part of raising our children and it is helpful to have some principles and guidelines to follow.

MAKE THE RULES CLEAR

Children need to understand where the limits lie in their behaviour and from an early age we must make clear what is and isn't allowed, and that obedience and defiance each have their consequences. Where are the boundaries for your child and what are the basics you expect?

Janet, mother of three and an experienced nursery nurse, suggested a few keys to communicating her basic rules to young children.

1. 'Always answer when your name is called and come straight away when asked. If I say "stop", do it at once' – excellent from a safety point of view as well as making everyday life easier.

2. 'Be gentle and polite.' Kicking, butting, pushing and other rough behaviour are not acceptable. We do not tolerate certain words, phrases or ways of talking to one another. 'I hate you!' for example, is just not on. While we want our children to be able to share openly how they think and feel, they must learn not to do so rudely or unkindly.

Dealing with cheekiness later will be easier if answering back and ungraciousness have been taught to be unacceptable from the beginning. A two-year-old telling you to 'Be quiet!' or 'Go away!' may sound cute, but it won't when she's four. A toddler can understand not to speak in that kind of way – although if you have older brothers and sisters giggling at the little one's antics the task is more difficult! And of course, if we want to instil politeness we need to treat them with respect and dignity even when we are angry and saying strong things. 'Please', 'I'm sorry', and 'Thank you' can be very early additions to a toddler's vocabulary. Although you will grow weary of prompting your children with these words, *it is worth it*. One day, they'll say it automatically!

3. 'Eat what is on your plate. When your first course is finished you can have your pudding.' Food is at the bottom of hundreds of rows between parents and children. If you can possibly steer a course through this issue you will save hours of aggravation.

4. 'Once in bed you stay there except for a very good reason.' Barring nightmares, being sick or some other disaster, there should be no getting up, and the same should apply to daytime sleeps. If you are not firm on this little visitors may regularly disturb your well-earned

evening off or hour's respite in the afternoon – and it can easily become a habit. For early wakers make a similar rule, that they stay in bed until you go in to them. Try putting a pile of books and even a biscuit and drink at their bedside once they have gone to sleep, to keep them happy through the early hours before breakfast time.

5. 'If you do as you are asked willingly, you will be rewarded and praised. If you wilfully disobey you will be told off and punished.' This simple choice is the key to all the others. Obviously we do not want mindless automatons with no originality or spark; there must be ample opportunities for children from the earliest age to express their individuality and experiment creatively. You need wisdom to know when it is appropriate to punish a child and what that punishment should be. There are some areas of behaviour where you should expect unquestioning and prompt obedience. Decide what these are and think of creative, unthreatening ways to persuade your child to conform. Don't feel you have to justify your decisions and actions to them all the time.

BE CONSISTENT, FIRM AND FAIR

Life with small children is so much easier if they really know that you mean what you say. So much time, emotional energy and words will be saved. We have all been panicked into promises that are impossible to fulfil, occasions when we have been pushed too far and threatened some totally over-the-top retribution the minute we get home. As a method of discipline, bribery, threats and heavy punishment are not to be recommended. They will not work in the long run, are morally suspect and won't deliver the self-discipline we hope will emerge as the child grows up.

So how should parents deal with misbehaving toddlers?

* *It is always best to be pro-active.* When you can foresee that she is likely to do something she knows is not allowed, act before it actually happens. Call her to you

before she heaves something at her brother, and firmly remind her about the rule you have about throwing things because they can do damage or hurt. Most children will respond and the moment can be changed from a telling-off to praise about how sensible she is.

* *Give him a chance.* Most misbehaviours are due to him not thinking or becoming over-excited. Intervene – 'I want you to sit quietly with me for a minute' – but not in 'punishment mode'. Explain that if he is too rough he will need to watch the other children play for a while, not join in.

* *Observe your child* so that you really understand why he does certain things that seem to be naughty. Before you get cross make sure you know exactly what is happening on the inside of him as well as the outside. Only correct mistakes when it is necessary and avoid inviting confrontation with a small child unless you really have to. Save it up for issues that really matter.

* *Watch out for those fragile times* when they are more likely to misbehave and you are more likely to over-react. Tiredness, staying in a home where you are not relaxed, packing before a holiday and Christmas are all pressure points.

* As a golden rule, *warn a child of punishment only if you are prepared to carry it out.*

Sammy was not having a good day. He wouldn't tidy his toys, wouldn't eat properly, wouldn't stand up to have his coat put on. He was driving Louise, his mum, crazy and it was only 8.30 in the morning. The long day stretched ahead ... 'If you aren't a good boy you won't go to Nicky's party this afternoon' seemed a good try at knocking some sense into his stubborn head. There was no change, Sammy was just in one of those moods and he couldn't pull out of it. Louise often repeated her threat during the morning but actually she had no intention of really keeping Sammy away from the party. The boy spent the day being impossible, screamed when she got his party clothes on and must have been very confused to find himself entertained, fed delicious food, getting presents and prizes and generally having a wonderful time. Louise had gambled and lost. She should never have suggested a punishment she was not really prepared to deliver. Instead of a positive lesson, Sammy learned that he doesn't really have to listen to what she says, Mum won't *really* punish him if he's naughty.

DON'T EXPECT THE IMPOSSIBLE

As adults, none of us does what is right all of the time. In the same way our children will never be perfectly behaved and should not be made to feel they lose anything of our love or affection when they fail to live up to our expectations.

Be careful not to demand impossible standards from a small child. Part of being a toddler is that things seem to happen around you. Milk spills, cupboards empty themselves all over the floor, floors become muddy and clothes sometimes get wet. It is very hard to remember instructions when your mind is on other important matters.

Then there is honesty. By the time children are about four or five, they will understand that it is wrong to tell a lie or take something that is not theirs. But a two- or three-year-old has not begun to grasp the meaning of truth or accept any concept of ownership. Gentle explanations can help the process start but it is not fair to punish a young toddler for stealing or lying.

FIND THE HAPPY MEDIUM

What do we expect of the under-fours? Some people, particularly in past generations, may have held very authoritarian views. There can be few miseries in life to compare eith a harsh upbringing when outward perfection is demanded by a parent, little affection and praise are given and rigid discipline rules the home. Inflicting this kind of regime on a child will inevitably cause emotional scars for life.

On a local bus I overheard the dreadful words of an agitated mother to a whining three-year-old: 'Stop it and shut up! Be careful or I won't love you any more and I'll give you away.' We rightly shudder to think of the long-term effect that kind of language has on a child, especially when he hears it often.

There is never any justification for a child to be punished – by word or deed – so that she is emotionally or physically damaged. If you find you can't help hurting your child when pressures get to you, please look for help before things get worse. More parents are in the same situation than you may think, and you can find the support you need.

There is no place for disciplining babies in any physical way. As they become old enough to play up you can communicate disapproval through facial expression, gestures, tone of voice.

At the other end of the discipline scale are those who seem to believe it wrong to correct children unless their behaviour is unsafe or anti-social. We have all suffered from other people's toddlers on the rampage and fumed as the parents have looked on benignly at their completely unrestrained offspring causing havoc. 'My boys are so highly strung, you know. I couldn't possibly stop them – it could do lasting psychological harm.' Mmmmmm.

True love is not spoiling them by giving in to every demand or ignoring naughty behaviour. It will sometimes mean being firm and sticking to your guns while at the same time you demonstrate patience and forgiveness.

Small children need to feel secure and able to trust in the people in their lives. Parents have the challenge of reinforcing that sense of security through words and actions. This includes correcting and disciplining them when necessary. We all lose our cool from time to time, approach situations unwisely and make bad mistakes.

It is not humanly possible to be a totally consistent parent all the time, always dependable to do exactly the right thing at the right time in the right way. Don't worry about it – we can only do the best we can in each situation that faces us day by day.

There's no such thing as 'failure' – only 'not got it quite right yet'. And that goes for children *and* parents.

13

WHERE THERE'S A WILL THERE'S A WON'T

Flopsy, Mopsy and Cotton-tail, who were good little bunnies, went down the lane to collect blackberries: but Peter, who was very naughty, ran straight away to Mr MacGregor's garden and squeezed under the gate!
The Tale of Peter Rabbit, Beatrix Potter

What can you do when a determined child wants something that you are not prepared to allow? When she weeps for those sweets placed tantalisingly by the supermarket checkout? If he wants to 'borrow' the breadknife to play pirates, she won't stop biting people or insists she is desperate to wear her best dress to the playground ...? The areas of conflict between a responsible parent and a single-minded toddler are infinite. But very often a cunning parent can win without the child ever realising it. The chief secret weapon in any child-carer's armoury is – diversion!

CREATING A DIVERSION

A baby who refuses to give you an object in his clenched hand will probably forget and drop it when offered something more interesting. Small children can only hold one thought in their mind at once – and distracting them can often save you from a confrontation.

There was a stick in the garden and two-year-old Helen was busy poking the cat with it. Her father asked her not to but she took no notice. This was a toddler on an all-absorbing mission and she was refusing to obey. However, as soon as Daddy suggested a drink in the kitchen Helen forgot the long-suffering tabby and made haste to the house!

Max was crying with anger because of a fight with his brother. He was also tired and did not resist when his dad sat him on his lap and started quietly to read a favourite book. Within a minute Max had dried his eyes so as not to miss this treat, and his tantrum was in the past.

Your first ploy as you reach the scene of a toddler trauma could be to stop dead and stare amazed into thin air. 'Good gracious! Did you see that?' 'What?' 'A huge green elephant just flew over the fence. He had a golden crown and was carrying some sticks in his trunk ...' Try it! If the fight/misdemeanour/tantrum was basically caused by boredom you might really start something creative and have a lot of fun. Make sure they understand you are pretending and not telling whopping great lies, though!

ENCOURAGING OBEDIENCE

As we have already seen, the best path to good behaviour is positive praise and loving encouragement.

But if your toddler is one of life's born fighters you will have your share of struggles as you bring her up. Console yourself that this strong personality will stand her in good stead when she faces her own crises in the future. Hang in there and don't give up on shaping the will – without crushing her spirit.

Maybe you are the proud parents of a cherub who is unfailingly sweet, cheerful, amenable and cute. Be thankful, but don't assume he will always be such a dream – be prepared for possible changes.

Most small children come somewhere in between, seeming to test out their adults occasionally to see if naughty, defiant behaviour really does matter, and most of the time responding readily to rewards, warnings and punishments.

With two- to three-year-olds the main issue at stake is obedience to our instructions versus their demands and getting their own way against our wishes. Start early, choose to tackle a few areas of behaviour and attitude at a time in order to build on them as time goes by, and patiently wait for improvement and change. This must always be in the context of our unconditional love.

Michelle was twenty months old. She could feed herself, managing cup, spoon and dish well. As the first pangs of hunger were satisfied, Michelle would slow down her eating and become more interested in dropping her food on the floor. Her mother, Liz, realised that the mess was not accidental and decided to put a stop to it. Easier said than done! It didn't help that the family dog loved to sit drooling and pleading beside Michelle's high chair, willing the baby to send down more delicious morsels! The first step was to keep the dog out at mealtimes. The next time Michelle was strapped into her chair for tea her mother told her firmly, looking into her eyes, 'Michelle! Don't drop food on the floor! *No!*' pointing to the food and the ground and shaking her head. Michelle listened and watched this solemnly, but as usual, after a minute or so began to empty her plate over the edge of her tray. Liz moved in. 'Michelle! No! No food on the floor!' and cleaned it up. Undeterred the toddler repeated her performance and her mother responded in stronger tones, wagging a finger and shaking her head (it helps to be something of an actress in this game!), and when Michelle persisted she said, 'Drop food on the floor and Mummy will take it away.' Michelle did, and, wishing she didn't have to, Liz carried out her promise and took the bowl of baked beans out of the room. Michelle cried, Liz kissed her fondly and repeated the formula. 'Michelle dropped food on the floor, Mummy took it away.' By now it was time for pudding which Liz spoon-fed to avoid further problems. At following meals this pantomime was repeated but within a few days Michelle abandoned her misdemeanour and the dog was allowed back in the kitchen!

Going through this kind of scene can be emotionally draining, time-consuming and tedious. But the issue at stake is not a dirty floor or wasted food so much as who is in charge of the relationship. Choose the things about which you are going to insist on compliance, concentrate on these and leave less important issues for another time.

Some children quickly conform and do not need to test out who's boss too often but there are many more who will take any and every opportunity to pit their will against yours, and if you value the prize of a child who will obey you rather than fight every instruction he is less than keen about, you will do your utmost to win those early battles. Be as positive and loving as you possibly can. It may take years; don't give up, it will be worth it in the end.

REWARDS

An old fable tells how Wind and Sun were boasting about their power one day and so decided on a contest to see who possessed the greater strength. Spotting a man walking along, Wind suggested the test should be to remove the coat he wore. Summoning his strongest gales, Wind set to work but his victim buttoned the coat up still more and was not parted from it. Breathless, Wind gave up and let Sun have a turn. Within minutes the intense heat persuaded the man to take off not only the coat but his shirt as well.

As parents we can sometimes be like Wind – wielding our authority to try to make a child do what we want. Shining is almost always more effective.

Awarding treats is an excellent practice and it is worth working out what best suits your family. There is a thin line to be drawn between unashamed bribery and the rewarding of good behaviour. We need to be careful that a sort of Infant Trades Union Movement does not invent itself and start insisting on chocolate as a pre-requisite to obedience.

Promising to stop at the ice-cream van later if everyone is good can lift sagging spirits, but be careful not to commit yourself to delivering rewards you regret afterwards. Are you sure you want the interior of the car covered in dribbly Mr Drippy ice-cream? Carrots to encourage human donkeys can be very simple – ten extra minutes in the playground, tea in the garden, 'phoning Granpa, feeding the ducks. While they are young, children won't realise you would probably do these things anyway and you can gain maximum benefit from your plans. Be careful, though; if Harry begins to play up, you may have to withdraw the treat you promised and although a trip to the pond would help everyone the project will have to be abandoned for that day.

KEEPING COOL

Most parents will freely confess to having shouted at their children sometimes. It usually happens when you are tired and when you fear things are sliding out of control. A feeling of panic suddenly appears from nowhere and perhaps you let rip in an effort to exert your authority. It is a horrible feeling and achieves little. When you realise you are losing your temper, it's wise to wait a few seconds or minutes and calm down a little. That way your reaction is not something you may regret later. And we should be willing to apologise to children when we get it wrong.

When you discipline a child it must be with self-control. Our emotions can be frighteningly powerful and it is possible to be like a sudden, avenging angel swooping down without warning. This is one reason for discussing ahead of time a suitable code of discipline for any given situation. Your thoughts at the time of confrontation may not be cool enough to be wise!

Your son or daughter must understand that certain actions or attitudes will always result in certain consequences! Warnings are good, but not threats – don't keep putting off the punishment hoping you won't have to carry it out. Let's face it, it is no fun dealing with naughty behaviour. If only it wasn't necessary.

And if only the need didn't arise at such awkward moments!

Flora wanted to go into the toyshop. Her parents were in a hurry to leave the shopping centre and get home. 'No, Flora. It's time to go,' they said. Flora started to cry, expertly working herself up into a full-scale tantrum while passers-by began to look on disapprovingly. The couple pressed on, trying to quieten the screaming child who was now shouting her demands at full volume. 'We'll have to do something,' muttered husband to wife, and just as they were debating what and where and how, who should be coming towards them but Aunt Vera, a disapproving sort of lady at the best of times and now looking totally scandalised at the dreadful performance before her horrified eyes. 'What is the matter, my darling Flora?' she cried. 'But of course you want to go to the toyshop and Auntie will buy you something.' Triumph gleamed in the child's eye and she stopped shrieking at once. Now what?

If Mummy and Daddy gave in to the unholy alliance of Auntie and Flora they would regret it. But the embarrassment of turning down Vera's offer, facing her offended retort, having to deal with a reactivated tantrum and then finding a discreet corner to give Flora a serious telling-off was no easy option either. Fortunately, just then, along came a man dressed in an oversized dog costume giving out pink balloons as part of a publicity exercise for a local business. Quick as a flash, Flora's mother drew her daughter's attention to this captivating sight and the tricky moment was overcome.

Parents naturally want to bring up their sons and daughters to do what is right, behave in an acceptable way, work to the best of their ability, make strong lasting relationships and fulfill the potential of their lives. Putting it into practice is not simple.

TO SMACK OR NOT TO SMACK?

Many believe it should be made illegal for parents to physically discipline their child. Champions of human rights, understandably concerned about the spiral of child abuse in the home, are eager to protect the young from harm. For some years now, corporal punishment in state schools has been banned. Concern about harsh, 'pin down' treatment of unruly children in care and locking them in their rooms dressed only in underclothes for days on end has highlighted this issue further.

There is a world of difference between angry beating and giving an unruly child a smack on his leg. You need not put these two actions in the same category and as a parent you may believe occasional physical discipline is appropriate. On the other hand the very idea may be repugnant to you and your opinion is that a spanking will do no good at all but lead your child to think that hitting is acceptable. This is a deeply personal issue and parents should think it through in relation to each individual case.

Some children cause no problems. They respond just to being 'told off' and when they deserve further punishment it is effective to send them off for a period or deprive them of a treat. Physically disciplining them is unnecessary and should be avoided.

But there are others who display extremely strong wills and tend to pit themselves against any and every instruction and boundary. Sooner or later the parent of such a child may resort to a smack. There are many who say it has a positive effect.

Tony described his son: 'Michael was really difficult. As a toddler and pre-school boy he constantly resisted any and every restraint put upon him.' The normal two-year-old stage of saying 'No!' to everything never went away and he became enmeshed in a cycle of negative behaviour and attitudes which was exhausting to deal with and made Michael unhappy too. 'We knew there were reasons for this which we worked to help him with but at the end of the day his behaviour had to be checked.'

Michael's mother tried everything. Her training as a primary teacher had taught her how children must find self-motivation, not be railroaded into learning but free to express their own individuality. Sure! – but young Michael was way past the limits and now, aged three-and-a-half, was rapidly controlling her! Tony, his dad, one of a big family brought up strictly but by very loving parents, saw the solution very simply; remembering how his dad dealt with any breach of good behaviour with a smack, he tried the same with Michael.

'I think it was the answer for Michael, he seemed almost relieved; it was the difference a thunderstorm makes on a muggy day.' Up until he was about six – after that they did not do it – a smack, given in private and followed by comfort and loving reassurance, helped him to overcome his stubborn disobedience.

RESPECTING THEIR DIGNITY

Jamie knew all right. He had been told enough times that helping himself to food from the fridge was a 'no-no'. When Dad caught him in the act of taking two cakes – one for himself and the other for his friend Yasmin – serious action was needed. 'Come with me, Jamie. I want to talk to you in the sitting room.' Jamie's playmate, his two sisters and Mum were left in the kitchen while father and son sorted things out privately.

* If at all possible, *try not to scold or punish a child in front of others*. Even if she doesn't express her embarrassment at being chastised in public she may be feeling keen embarrassment. At home, take her to another room – the walk gives you a minute to collect your thoughts and decide what to say and do.

* *Watch your words*. Hate the sin and not the sinner, trying not to attack the child but express your objection to his

behaviour. Even if you decide to banish him to his room for ten minutes, make it clear that you still love him even if you don't like the way he's acting.

* *Comparisons are odious.* The relationship between young friends or brother and sister will not be improved if you point out how good the one is and how awful the other. Even if you think it, try not to say it – either directly to your children or to someone else in their hearing.

* *Never belittle a child.* They are, after all, very small and vulnerable and in the heat of the moment and in our exasperation at monstrous behaviour we long to retaliate. Keep away from degrading punishments or insulting words. Even in your anger, love must still be there.

KISS AND MAKE UP

Sarah and young Natalie glared at each other. The little girl had gone too far, been rude to her mum once too often. 'Don't you ever say those words to me again!' Sarah told her rebellious three-year-old standing there with furrowed brow and down-turned mouth. 'Sorry,' Natalie growled and the tears sprouted from her eyes. Sarah sighed, put out her arms and drew her daughter close. 'I love you, darling, please try not to talk like that again.' The arms went round her neck and squeezed. 'I love you too, Mummy.'

When the incident is over, never fail to take your child on to your lap and reassure her of your love and forgiveness; that it is the behaviour you dislike, not her. Learning about reconciliation, apology and forgiveness is a wonderful lesson that most of us find hard. Try to help your small children to accept it early by your love and reassuring response to their wrongdoings.

Various methods of revenge and retribution flashed through her head the day Stella discovered Lucy (three-and-a-half), a dripping brush and a tin half full of pink gloss paint (left with lid loosely fitted in the cupboard under the stairs). The freshly decorated bedroom with its new carpets and curtains was daubed with streaks of 'Summer Rose'.

But Stella managed to weigh her words carefully before she actually spoke!

'Mummy loves you but is very, very, very cross with you,' she told her 'darling' daughter. 'You have done a very naughty thing and I am going to punish you for making such a dreadful mess in here. Do you want to say something to me?'

Stella can't work it out to this day. Was Lucy being remarkably obtuse or incredibly cunning? Chin trembling and china-blue eyes saucer-wide she answered, 'But Mummy! I did it for you because you love pink best!'

Everyone makes mistakes, we will all lose our tempers and experience bad days! Life with pre-school children is not a soft option and if we take the challenge seriously to love and train them, our patience, ingenuity, generosity and sense of humour will be tested to the uttermost.

But are there any guarantees that our kids will turn out OK? Can we discover a child-rearing formula that produces perfect people? No. At the end of the day, we can only do our very imperfect best to love, train and shape our children from the earliest age and eventually let them loose to lead their own lives.

14

PART OF THE FAMILY

The best gift we can give our children is a stable, caring
and loving family and a secure home to live in. Not that
such families don't have problems, but at least they
share a commitment to solving whatever difficulties
arise, come what may.

Sir Harry Secombe, Patron, National Family Trust

Living with children of any age provides a ringside seat to
observe human behaviour and relationships in the raw.
Your family circus will be well in progress by the time the
children reach two or three years old. Those pure and
innocent newborn babies gradually develop into less than
perfect toddlers who at the drop of a hat can perform
quite amazing turns – tantrums, war games and other
dramas. Even compliant members of the family have their
moments.

CHANGING TIMES

Of course it is not always that eventful, but most of our lives
are far from the idealised picture of the classic TV advertisement for breakfast cereals, where Mr and Mrs Perfect sit
serenely smiling at their immaculate 2. 4 children in a
spotless kitchen with a gleaming Volvo estate in the
drive. Real families have more to do with grumpy toddlers
with runny noses, toys strewn underfoot, mislaid belongings, lost library books and a clapped-out car which may
not start at crucial moments!

However imperfect, the family has always been the basic building block of any successful society. It is important to encourage and support the traditional pattern of husband, wife and children supported by extended family members, but at the same time to recognise the significant changes of the last few generations.

An increasing number of households include step-children, many families are headed by a lone parent and have every chance of raising happy, well-adjusted children while 'traditional' ones may not. What is certain is that being a parent today is more of a challenge than ever before.

The enormous changes in recent years have contributed to social breakdown of all kinds.

* Lone-parent households make up almost one fifth of families with dependent children.
* More than a quarter of babies are born outside of a marriage relationship.
* Each week the parents of almost 350 children under sixteen divorce. Britain has one of the highest rates of divorce in western Europe.
* Divorces and separations cost the government around £3 million each year in welfare, legal and other costs.

We have yet to understand fully the causes and effects of social change. It has been estimated that by the end of the century only about half of all British children will experience conventional family lives – parents married at the time they were born and continuing married until they are grown up. How well will the current generation of children cope with parenting the next?

EXTENDED FAMILIES

Most of us, if we could choose, would opt for a stable, loving partnership of mother and father where children have the best chance of a balanced, secure upbringing, supported by a wider clan – grandparents, aunts, uncles and cousins, who are all important to give support, variety and a sense of belonging to a wider group of people. But for a growing number of people, life is just not like that and many parents are called upon to make a super-human effort to provide for and nurture their families without the support of a partner or even other members of the family.

However, extended families can have their drawbacks! Well-meaning mothers-in-law, better behaved cousins and easily offended great aunts make up the tapestry of many a family! But if your parents, brothers, sisters and other relatives want to be involved, make the most of it! Grandparents have a special role to play and can be extremely important to young children. Grandmothers and grandfathers have more time and are often good at making things, answering difficult questions and listening to your little ones prattle on. You may have had to move away because of employment demands but the value of those blood ties is priceless; the continuation of the generations has much to offer to the well-being of our communities, rural and urban.

BROTHERS AND SISTERS

Families are where we learn how to relate to other human beings. It is fascinating to see how different two children in a family can be. Same parents, same child-rearing methods, same environment – and yet they are like chalk and cheese.

Newborns are bundles of surprises, some of which will not be discovered for years to come. In the early years the basic personality emerges and sometimes clashes with others in the family. Siblings are particularly useful for playing with and carrying out experiments on. Many a toddler has had to suffer the indignities of an older child bossing her about. Competition, about everything and anything, is rife and parents begin to count the hours to bedtime.

SIBLING SQUABBLES

'It's my book, give it to *me*!'

'No! It's *mine*!'

'I want it! I want it! Mummeee!'

'Mummy! Make her give me my book!'

You wearily regard this typical squabble between brother and sister in the driving mirror. You are on the way to the swimming pool for a treat which is not working out as happily as planned. You are feeling jaded already and haven't even got to the undressing yet, never mind the armbands that won't blow up – or the swim itself. Then you'll have to cope with them dripping and fractious, whining for drinks and biscuits and taking ages to get dressed!

Why, you wonder, argue over a book which neither of them actually wants to read? Why can't these two people you love so very much get on with each other? By now, things are going from bad to worse, in fact World War Three is about to break out in the back of the car, each tugging at a dog-eared Ladybird book, bought for five pence at a jumble sale and until today, totally ignored. Title: *We Have Fun!* If only, you reflect grimly.

It's called sibling rivalry and it happens in most healthy families. At times like these, tell yourself that you are going to be able to stop this situation, you are in control. Keep even the hint of a plea or panic from your voice. And after the event – but soon enough for it to be fresh in their memories – talk about the need to share, say sorry, be kind, etc., etc. Insist they say 'Sorry' and 'That's all right' to each other and then try to lighten the whole atmosphere and move them on to something new. Being a peace negotiator is a tough and a frequent role in parenting! Jealousy, feelings of inadequacy, personality differences, tiredness, secret grudges or just plain awkwardness all contribute to sibling rivalry. Try not to take it too much to heart.

Little children need to be shown how to solve conflicts, resolve upsets and mend bruised relationships. Many adults never had that advantage and are socially handicapped to this day! Try to recognise what is happening when there is an argument going on, to know how best to intervene. Some rough and tumble between young children is just a learning process or a bit of amusement when they are bored.

Two-and-a-half-year-old Jessie and her older brother get on well. Generally they play happily together with their toys or immerse themselves in games of imagination but sometimes, as if by mutual agreement, they pick a fight with each other, becoming quite heated about the issue at stake. Their mother recognises that this bickering is merely another form of play. Unless it goes on too long or becomes unpleasant she leaves them to sort themselves out. If they are squabbling over a particular object, she might take it away and say that neither child may have it. Wisdom and experience will grow and a sense of humour is invaluable!

TWINS

There they are, like two peas in a pod dressed in their pretty pink pramsuits, side by side in their double buggy. So fascinating and appealing – twins!

'The first six months was a nightmare. We never seemed to rest. I was exhausted from feeding them both.' Non-stop hard work, but worth it all – twins! If you are the proud parents of twins, you deserve all the encouragement and praise that is going!

1. *Contact TAMBA* – The Twins and Multiple Births Association. This is the affiliation of all the Twin Clubs and other support groups around the country. Joining one is a very good idea. The Multiple Births Foundation, based at Queen Charlotte's Hospital, London, is another key organisation, promoting knowledge about twins to professionals (teachers, doctors, social workers, etc.) and parents.

2. If *routine* is important when you have one baby, it is tantamount to survival for the parents of twins. Prepare the

whole day's supply of milk at the same time each morning, be as organised as possible about washing, shopping and cooking.

3. *Prioritise*. There is too much to do, so decide what is important and cut corners on the rest. Don't iron anything unless it is vitally necessary, and if you can afford it, use ready-made baby food rather than cooking your own. Beware of feeling guilty about the things you cannot do!

4. *Treat them as individuals*. Obviously for much of the time you will care for twins as one unit. They will be good company for each other from earliest babyhood. But as they grow, take time with each individual, try not to refer to them as 'the twins' and discourage others from labelling them like that too. Avoid dressing them the same and look out for ways they express their own individuality wherever possible. Spend time alone with each child, help them have their own friends as well as joint ones and sometimes do activities separately even though it will be more time-consuming!

5. *Enlist help!* Wider family involvement will make all the difference. Accept any support that is offered! Try to have a regular window of free time for yourself. It will ward off insanity!

6. *Pre-school education* is particularly important for twins, especially if they are very dependent on one another. The more friends they have the better. When they start school, consider having them in separate classes if possible.

A NEW BABY

Imagine the shock to a two-year-old who has always enjoyed the sole rights to her parents' affection and attention, when a dear little baby brother appears. All at once, this screaming person, who can't even play with her properly, takes up residence on her mother's lap, commandeers her old cot and charms every visitor to the house and anyone they meet.

However carefully parents prepare an older child for the arrival of the next, there will be difficult adjustments, and mixed in with the joy and celebration long-lasting jealousies and resentments which, unchecked, can go on for years. Some situations are more difficult than others and it is not always easy to recognise how a child is reacting.

Pippa and Nick were expecting their second baby and were so excited that everyone knew about it within days of the positive pregnancy test. Eighteen-month-old Freddie soon picked up the 'vibes' that something was going on and as time went by and he entered that wonderful stage, called by some the 'terrible twos', he became less and less easy to manage. His parents puzzled over the change and privately wondered how they would cope with two children!

It was fixed that when Pippa went into hospital, Freddie would go and sleep with his cousins. Unfortunately it was two in the morning when they woke him and drove him there and he was not too happy. The next day he visited his new brother but was quite unprepared for the unfamiliar surroundings of the hospital ward. He saw his mum and ran to have a cuddle but she seemed too busy with this white bundle of blanket which made a funny noise. When he tried to see what it was he was told sharply not to touch, and was ignored by everyone.

Spot the mistakes! None of them deliberate, I am sure, but all destined to produce endless trouble for Freddie and his family. Toddlers need handling very carefully and there are plenty of positive ways in which they can be helped to understand and accept this new person – who after all threatens to topple the older child from his throne and steal his parents' love and attention.

1. *Tell your toddler* about the new baby a few months before the birth. Explain it in the simplest of terms and let him feel the kicking baby inside you. He can become involved in the fun of preparation and finding baby clothes and equipment.

2. *Reassure him* of your continuing and unabated love. Step up positive praise but be careful not to worry your child that he will be expected to be more sensible and grown up than he feels he can. His role as Mummy's helper needs to be seen as fun and he needs to understand that the promised 'little brother or sister to play with' will start off by being rather a demanding and rather boring infant. You could visit a friend's baby to see what it was like. If possible let him see inside the hospital a few weeks before the baby is due. 'This is where Mummy and Daddy will come when the baby is ready to be born and you will go up in this lift when you come to see your baby.'

3. *Decide and explain well ahead of time who will look after your child*, and where, when the time comes. It is probably ideal to let him stay at home, with a grandma or some other familiar figure to come and stay. If he will be in someone else's house, consider a trial run some weeks before the event.

4. *The first sight of the baby is crucial.* Try to make sure that the newborn is not in Mummy's arms – she is still there for the older child. Give more cuddles and hugs to your older one than usual, not less. Reassure him that he is just as special as he has always been. Make out that the baby really loves him. A present from the newborn is a good plan, and interpret smiles and other charming behaviour as friendliness directed to a big brother.

5. *Encourage adults to pay particular attention* to the older child when they visit the baby. Once home, carve out time alone to talk, cuddle, play and read and involve him in as much of the babycare as possible.

6. *Watch for the times he wants to pretend* to be a baby and play along with it. Reverting to thumb-sucking, bed-wetting, baby talk and wanting to drink from a bottle are all signs of this, he is making sure of your attention and love. Don't worry or over-react, just try to use every opportunity to give extra affection and praise.

7. *Your toddler could feel very disconcerted* to find the new baby is taking over *his* belongings. Make sure that he is transferred to a 'big boy's bed' long before the other one needs the cot. You could approach this issue by maintaining that it is *his* cot which he is kindly lending to the baby.

If, despite all your efforts, the older one feels seriously displaced, how is he likely to express his feelings?

* Plain speaking – 'I want the baby to go away.'
* Physical attack – poking, pushing, etc. (never leave them together unattended, just in case).
* Acting like a baby himself – reverting to thumb-sucking, needing a nappy, waking at night, talking baby language, etc.
* Naughty behaviour, gaining attention and testing adult response.
* Becoming withdrawn.
* Being excessively attentive to the baby – trying to deny true feelings and guilt.

This stage will probably pass naturally. Even if he is trying your patience, try to understand what is happening and deal with each day as calmly and lovingly as you can.

Of course, if and when your third child comes along, you may have to go through this all over again! Happy parenting!

15
HIGH DAYS AND HOLIDAYS

Whether the weather be fine
Or whether the weather be not
Whether the weather be cold
Or whether the weather be hot -
We'll weather the weather
Whatever the weather
Whether we like it or not!

Anon

Before having children, how you spend your free evenings, weekends and holidays is largely your own choice; a welcome opportunity to relax and do your own thing. But once a baby's in the picture options are seriously reduced! Even a trip to the cinema or to visit friends needs strategic planning. You must first find a suitable babysitter – which may add to the evening's expenses before you start! – and only when you feel sure your child is in the right frame of mind to be left for these precious few hours can you escape together and be yourselves for just a couple of hours! But do your best to spend time together away from home as often as you can – even if it is just for a walk and a coffee out somewhere.

ESCAPING

* Family! Some children have the great fortune to have grandparents living nearby who are able and happy to be with them. Make the most of any offers to help.

* Friends! Having someone else's child over to play can be easier than having your own alone. And hopefully, a few days later the arrangement will work the other way to give you a couple of child-free hours. You might even try the odd sleep-over, but only when you are confident that your son or daughter will be quite comfortable and secure away from home.

* Fathers! Why not take the children away on a Saturday for a couple of hours to the swimming pool, playground – *anywhere* away from your partner – and give her some breathing space? You could even give her a lie in and breakfast in bed! Remember, she is probably never in the house without the children.

Weekends, especially for mothers, whether they stay home with the children or work outside the home all week long, are hard work. Little children have to be entertained, watched and cared for 365 days a year. Chores need doing and commitments have to be met. Parents rarely have days off, and can't even be ill in bed, without the support of others!

The more you can talk through the issues and plan child-friendly activities to share in and enjoy together, the better. Make contingency plans for emergency situations and think about the implications of invitations and events that include your under-fives.

DAYS OUT

Gemma was to be a bridesmaid just a week before her fourth birthday. At last her lifelong ambition was to be realised! – she couldn't wait for that moment of glory when everyone would admire the flowers in her hair and the long floaty dress tied with a velvet sash. Her parents were almost as excited as Gemma and they too were looking forward to their young family meeting the wider clan of uncles, aunts and other relations who would also be at the wedding.

The present was wrapped, the confetti bought and everyone had been kitted out in their best clothes. The family drove to church, dropping over-excited Gemma off on the way and Phil and Jacqui looked forward to the day. Unfortunately the baby started crying during the vows and had to be taken out by Jacqui, and as his mother disappeared, Tom the toddler also began to wail. Why is life so complicated when you have a couple of little ones? Anyway, Gemma enjoyed her day and looked wonderful and the photographs were lovely ...

Don't underestimate the amount of organisation it will take to get your show on the road for a day out. It is as well not to be too ambitious, although there are couples who have sailed the Atlantic with a few toddlers as crew and plenty of families manage to travel without major traumas. But it is as well to be prepared.

HOLIDAYS

Holidays with children are different.

Heidi was completely unprepared for the disappointment of that first summer holiday with her twins. She and her husband had looked forward for weeks to their return to the Greek islands where they had honeymooned, far from the pressures of ordinary life. They had somehow overlooked the fact that the two major stresses in their life were coming with them this time!

Choose holidays to suit your children and don't *expect* to have a break yourself. Think carefully about the merits of self-catering versus hotel accommodation, or even camping.

Seek advice from other families who have trodden this route for years already!

* With small children avoid hot climates and only plan very long journeys if absolutely crucial.
* Pack carefully. It is frustrating to be without equipment you really need. On the other hand, it is all too easy to take too much! Phone beforehand to check what is available at your holiday accommodation.
* If you plan to buy a special toy for Christmas or a birthday, consider giving it to your child for the holiday if it is a manageable size! If as parents you can maximise on the novelty value, you may enjoy a little more peace!
* Pack paperback books and consider a cassette player with story tapes for rest and sleep times. New colouring and drawing materials are a good idea.
* It *is* possible for you *each* to have a little time to yourselves. For an hour and a half each day one of you can disappear while the other prevents the baby from swallowing stones and dipping her sandwiches in the sea. Then you can swap!
* Prepare a small well-stocked first aid kit. Make sure to take and use sunscreen for your children and monitor their exposure to the sun. You may need to treat sunburn, insect bites, tummy bugs, fever or minor cuts and bruises. It is no fun trying to explain what you need to puzzled-looking pharmacists in foreign parts!
* Accept the fact that family holidays are different and you will find they can be enjoyable. Try and slip away for a weekend alone later in the year while Granny minds the children.

BIRTHDAYS

Birthdays are wonderful opportunities to make people feel loved and valued. Children derive particular satisfaction from this special day when they are at the centre of attention. How can you best celebrate this important landmark, making your child feel special without over-doing the treats and spoiling him? Children's parties don't have to be complicated or expensive. The thought of all those party bags, spilled fizzy drinks and the expectations of over-excited guests may put you off the idea of celebrating your children's birthdays in style, but do not be intimidated – it can be fun!

* The first birthday can be very simple. Your baby is oblivious to the fact that he has reached this important landmark, so if you wish, just invite some friends for a tea party and put toys on the floor to amuse the younger guests.

* Is your child a party type or would she actually prefer a special outing with just one friend? How about a trip to the zoo, the seaside, the theatre or a film?

* You can host the party at home – probably easier for the first few years. This will be cheaper, and more comfortable for the parents who stay with their off-spring. Don't be too ambitious; eight or ten will be quite enough to handle. Send out invitations for twelve because a couple are bound to be unable to come.

* Alternatively, for three-year-olds upwards, choose an outside venue. Swimming pools, fast food restaurants, church halls and parks are all possible sites. Bouncy castles are good for the super-energetic – with proper supervision of course. Fancy dress, professional enter-tainment or good old 'The farmer's in his den' type games can keep the children amused for the hour or two they are in your care and not eating.

* Many parents combine their child's party with a friend's. If the birthday dates are close together and the children share many friends, why not?

* Unless you really love doing it, don't spend hours preparing beautiful food. If we're honest, children like crisps and chocolate biscuits more than anything.

Pieces of fruit, cubes of cheese, slices of pizza and sausages could be served first before all the crispy snacks. Make sure anything sweet is kept out of sight until the savouries have been eaten.

* A custom-built birthday cake can be a lovely way to make your child feel special. It doesn't matter much how it tastes but the more spectacular in appearance the better! They are much easier to make than you might think. You can easily find cook books with good ideas and simple instructions.

Don't feel you'll have to be a cross between Supercook, Mr Moneybags and Coco the Clown to make your child's birthday party a success. Just relax, watch the costs and enjoy it! Your child certainly will.

CHRISTMAS

Ask most children what they like about Christmas and if they are honest they'll say, 'Presents!' We may talk till the cows come home about giving and sharing with others, especially reminding them of whose birthday it is anyway, but the season is in danger of being spoilt by their preoccupation with all they hope to get! It is hardly our children's fault – the hype begins in October, with alluring advertisements on television, visions of Santa Claus and the mounting excitement and busyness going on around them.

How can we do our best to help our children value the true meaning and joy of Christmas and avoid the over-excitement?

1. *Plan ahead.* If they do too much the over-excitement and tiredness will spoil Christmas for you all. Make sure there are a few quiet days even if it means missing a party or two.

Making Christmas cards or gift tags from the ones you received last year is fun – or you can buy them ready for colouring in.

2. *Children adore putting up the decorations*, but for the sake of sanity remember to check them out first! It is frustrating enough trying to make fairy lights work anyway, without an eager three-year-old desperate to 'help'! Young children will probably be satisfied with hanging a few balls on the tree. If you can spare it, give them some tinsel and unbreakable decorations to put in their own room. Making paper chains is excellent too (cheap, time-consuming and makes minimal mess!).

There are extra safety risks at Christmas. Electric leads, candles, breakable ornaments and tasty-looking holly berries are hazardous to little ones. Talk to them about the dangers and keep them away unless you are watching.

3. *Do not let standards of behaviour drop* because it's Christmas. Try to keep a normal routine as far as possible – late bedtimes usually result in grumpy children and too much change can make them feel a little insecure and be wearing on adult nerves.

4. *There are wonderful programmes on television* over Christmas. Not only will they enjoy watching but you can have a break! But think carefully how much, when and for how long! If you can video programmes, do. Small children should not watch for too long a spell. After half an hour, a two-year-old should be removed, to be involved in another activity. Talk about what they watch and try to make it a shared experience, not a silent isolated one. Children of three and four will probably manage longer – but when it's time to switch off, be firm! Warn them in advance.

5. *A real dilemma* for some parents is whether children should be told the awful truth, that Father Christmas is not real. Santa is firmly in the centre of our Christmas celebrations and turns up everywhere. Is it best to make it plain to the very youngest child that he isn't real? Should we go along with the story, leave out a tasty snack on Christmas Eve and pretend Father Christmas *was* the one who gave them their presents? Is it right to expect small

children to learn to be honest and believe our words if we then tell them things which are not true?

One solution is to say to children from about three, 'Father Christmas isn't real – he's just a story. But let's pretend!' This way you can enjoy the fun, explain why he looks slightly different each time they see him – in a shop, on a film, visiting the nursery school or at a party – and help them begin to distinguish between fantasy and fact.

6. *Space out the presents*, especially if your child has a lot to open. Choose which ones to have on Christmas Day and let them open one or two each day, before the twenty-fifth and afterwards. They will appreciate each gift far more than if every package is ripped open in an orgy of having. Once your child is old enough, make sure she understands who has given each present and help her to say thank you. Babies will often enjoy the wrappings more than what is inside.

7. *Build family traditions*. Build up a collection of books about Christmas saved specially for December. Each year the wonderful story of Bethlehem can come alive again. Your two-year-olds may love the lambs and the donkey, at three talk about the baby Jesus, and by four find the idea of all those angels and the big star really exciting. Take plenty of time out to discover the story of Christmas with your toddler and pre-school child. There are all the cards to look at, Christmas carols to sing, and perhaps your family has a set of figures to set up depicting the stable scene. Hanging up stockings, reading the Christmas story together, special food ... whatever it is for you, encourage each new child to feel part of Christmas. It will be one of his most vivid memories when he grows older. Build up some family traditions.

Christmas is a celebration which focuses on childhood. It is a special time for expressing our love and appreciation to others, and the greatest pleasure for many is to see the delight and pleasure Christmas brings to children. A highlight of the season for many a doting parent is the Nativity

Play! Those little voices singing 'Away in a Manger' and the dramatic effect of all the shepherds and angels dressed in tea towels and tinsel reduces many a doting mum to tears.

Liz and Jackie decided to produce a Christmas play in playgroup. They worked hard on the casting, choreography, music and costumes. The smallest children (one was only eighteen months) were dressed in an assortment of tutus, sheepskin waistcoats, cotton wool and coat-hangers, either as lambs or as the heavenly host. There were shepherds and a trio of kings wearing cut-down cocktail dresses and paper crowns. Mary and Joseph, both just three, promised to be sensible. By the day of the performance emotions were running high. One of the kings didn't turn up but the show had to go on. Everything went well to start with. Some sheep suffered stage fright and wanted their mummies and a couple of cherubs fell off the platform – or were they shoved? – but nobody was injured and the sub-plot all added to the developing drama centre stage.

Feeling a little grumpy that morning, the Virgin Mary had flatly refused to wear her cornflower blue dress so she sat next to Joseph clad only in vest, tights and a net curtain. After a while two kings arrived with some presents but much to everyone's surprise, Joseph decided to unwrap them. Once opened the gifts were rather disappointing, so he stuffed one of them, the myrrh jar, with some straw from the crib, and leaned over to empty it out over Mary's head. An argument broke out, some shepherds joined in and the holy moment was lost in merriment and laughter both on and off stage. Liz and Jackie should have won an Oscar, it was wonderful and summed up some of the difficulties of raising under-fives!

Christmas is a reminder of the miracle of new life and the precious gift of a child. The coming of Jesus was unique, of course, and we might think of Mary and Joseph as extraordinary parents, but after all, every parent is special, and the birth of each baby is a holy event.

16
ALL THINGS BRIGHT AND BEAUTIFUL

All things bright and beautiful,
All creatures great and small,
All things wise and wonderful,
The Lord God made them all.

Mrs C. F. Alexander

'Mummy! Daddy! I found a poor dead rainbow lying in the road!' The four-year-old boy was almost in tears to have made such a sad discovery in a puddle on a busy city street. He had heard the story of Noah's ark and how God put a rainbow in the sky as a sign of his promise of forgiveness. He remembered seeing rainbows himself as the sun shone through the rainfall. But now he was shocked to find this glimpse of heaven suddenly brought down to earth – a spillage of oil floating in some muddy water. He was right, it did look like a dead rainbow. How did his parents find the right words to respond to his dismay? Besides a factual explanation, this child needed a different kind of reassurance. He had unwittingly stumbled on the realisation that the bright and beautiful in life can be spoiled. Something deep inside him that he couldn't quite understand yet had been alerted – his spirit.

NURTURING SPIRITUAL AWARENESS

Nurturing spiritual awareness and moral understanding is very important. We want the child's innermost spirit to grow, absorbing the wonder of life and wondering at its joy and sadness. As they live through certain events – the death of a friend, a neighbour or a grandparent for example – we can help them to unpack their thoughts and feelings and lay foundations which have the capacity to develop and mature into adult faith and moral understanding.

The dictionary defines the spirit as the vital animating essence of an individual – it's the real person inside. We all have an inbuilt urge to seek a deeper reality in our everyday lives and different people discover it in different ways and places. Our spiritual awareness evolves from early childhood onwards.

This is, of course, a very personal issue; what fits one family's values and lifestyle may be more difficult for another. For Lyndon and me, our Christian faith is central to all we do – and that includes parenthood.

FINDING FAITH

Britain today enjoys a rich diversity of racial, cultural and religious differences, but most of the population consider themselves Christian because of the past history, culture and institutions of our national life. In school, children receive religious education from a broadly Christian perspective which, opinion polls confirm, is what the majority of parents want. Society may appear more concerned with material wealth and happiness than with thinking about God, but increasing numbers are taking another look. Many churches will be filled this Sunday with people seeking and finding authentic spiritual truth that is real and relevant. Church attendance is higher now than it was fifty years ago. This growing interest in spiritual life is reflected in other religious communities in Britain as well.

For many people the experience of having a baby and sharing in his growth is an exciting spiritual adventure in itself. Questions about life and its meaning somehow take on a fresh importance as they witness the new life of their child.

Vicky felt that month by month a fundamental change was coming over her. The outside signs of her pregnancy were obvious enough – but deep within her also swelled an extraordinary sense of jubilation about the new person growing inside her body. She'd sit and imagine what the baby was like and wonder at how it had been made, the bones, muscles, heart and brain so secretly growing – a tiny miracle. Vicky wanted to pray, although she had always thought she didn't really believe in God. As the weeks passed she wondered how to find out more and thought about going to church.

Where parents have strong beliefs, these will usually be a significant influence on the way they bring up a child. The vast majority of parents who have their babies baptised are not regular church-goers but accept this tradition for the sake of their children. Others have never gone in for church-going and feel uncomfortable about having their babies christened. And there are those who are unsure about *what* they think and are searching for spiritual reality that is relevant and makes sense.

LEARNING ABOUT RIGHT AND WRONG

Princess Grace of Monaco once made a very wise comment:

> Many parents do nothing about their children's religious education, telling them to decide what they believe when they're twenty-one. That's like telling them they can decide when they are twenty-one, whether or not they should brush their teeth. By then, their teeth may have fallen out. Likewise, their principles and morality may also be non-existent. (Taken from *The Gift of a Child*, Marion Stroud, Lion, 1982)

The most effective way for us to help children know right from wrong and respond to the promptings of their consciences is by talking about it in ways they can grasp.

For Christians, right and wrong is interlinked with belief and trust in a God who has created everything and everyone, has given us his laws to live by and who shows love, forgiveness and mercy in the light of our human weakness. Knowing God can be an integral part of our lives, not an extra, holy layer to make us be or feel good. As a child grows old enough to grasp the idea, she can begin to understand that Christianity teaches us that some words and actions are wrong and others are good. Encouraging her to respect and care for others, saying 'thank you', 'please', and 'sorry', can all be grounded on simple spiritual truths. A Christian family will pray with their children from time to time, introduce them to the Bible and meet to worship with others in church. Where does it start?

BEFORE BIRTH

Unborn children are susceptible to all kinds of influences – and the very way we express love in that pre-birth period will have a positive spiritual effect. You may choose to ask sympathetic friends or family members to join with you as parents praying through the pregnancy, simply asking God to keep the baby from harm, for development to proceed normally and praying about the future too.

BABES IN ARMS

The gospels describe Jesus taking children in his arms and blessing them. For a religious leader to act like this was totally at odds with the conventions of his culture and he scandalised many of the people who watched him do it. The most natural and effective way of communicating love to a young baby is by holding, caressing, rocking and gently speaking to her. Jesus touched and embraced those children as he blessed them. The sense of belonging and security is crucial to our emotional well-being and success in life. Jesus would not be stopped from reaching out affectionately to express his physical and spiritual love to little children.

If we had been there that day and managed to place our babies into Jesus' arms to receive a blessing, how would we have felt? Christian families worship Jesus as the one who longs to bless our children still, as part of the natural development taking place in the whole of their lives. The spiritual care of a small baby – the communication of secure acceptance, through touch, voice, gentleness and being there – is natural and vitally important. Research has shown that young babies deprived of close warm affection will not only fail to thrive emotionally but also lack physical health and strength. Some parents will pray with and for their children – at bedtime, during the night when they are asleep or at family mealtimes. When they are ill or upset for some reason, Christian parents will often dispense prayer along with Calpol or a sticking plaster to help them recover. Without overdoing it or being trivial this can aid them to regard God as an accepted central part of their lives – there at all times. Of course babies do not understand, or particularly notice, when we pray for them but it can become part of the routine they are growing up to expect.

TODDLERS

As children emerge from babyhood, their comprehension of the world around them begins to take shape. They are completely egocentric – life revolves around them. Their people, places, belongings and memories seem like so many planets winging their way around the sun of self. Moving from this delusion towards the rather disappointing realisation that they are actually only one tiny part of creation rather than its epicentre takes time. Alas, some of us adults do not appear to have understood this yet.

Toddlers are learning that everything has its own name and separate identity. As they get older, children begin to think about things they cannot actually see, and start to discover very simple examples of the laws of cause and effect.

A two-year-old's understanding about God will be very primitive – and often very amusing. She will be a long way from being able to make real sense of complicated concepts and ideas such as praying or dying or going to heaven, but as children enter the toddler stage, there are various ways to communicate spiritual truths in a manner that fits their immaturity and delightful innocence. Be relaxed about it. Children who have experienced it from birth, accept an adult praying for them as nonchalantly as having their buttons done up! Perhaps you and your family do not operate like that but even if up until now there has not really been a spiritual dimension to everyday life, don't worry – children of any age are open to the truth about God, provided it is presented to them in a sincere and relevant way.

When Don and Marie's son and daughter were small they started praying with them and reading Bible stories with them very naturally in the early mornings, snuggling up together in bed with a cup of tea. (The sheets used to get really messy but it made for a great feeling of togetherness.) It was short and sweet; a story, a song and a three-line prayer from Mummy or Daddy asking Jesus to take care of them all. By the age of four, both children could pray about a given topic, choose a song and say what they liked about the Bible story they had just read. At times it felt mechanical, sometimes it bordered on the irreverent, but real understanding and spiritual experience was later built on these basic foundations.

Nought to five are the important foundation-laying years for parents to talk about these things, and others can help too – children's activities are run in almost every local church, and even if you do not wish to attend services yourself, they may be quite happy to accept your children and teach them the simple beliefs of Christianity in a caring, educational way. If you are already part of a church, remember that Sunday school programmes best build on what children learn at a parent's knee.

QUESTIONS YOU WISH THEY WOULDN'T ASK

It would be fun to put together an anthology of the wonderful comments and questions young children come out with. Some of the best are centred round religious ideas.

'Does Jesus sleep in a bunk bed like me?'

'Does he have a teddy or shall I lend him mine?'

'Why does God's house have such funny coloured windows with no curtains?'

'Jesus' angels have come to tea and they want strawberries as well.'

'Is heaven in Disney World?'

'When I say things to God, he doesn't say things back.'

Some of the questions three- and four-year-olds come up with are unanswerable for adults – let alone small children. It can be quite unsettling to have them ask about sensitive issues like death and the suffering of someone who is sick or in trouble. We will obviously shield very young children from some of the sadnesses and harsh realities of life, but there are times for simple honesty.

William was very fond of his grandmother. She had often looked after him ever since he was a baby, and for his third birthday in August she had baked him a beautiful cake that looked just like a racing car. He hadn't seen her much since then, although now it was nearly Christmas – Daddy said she wasn't very well and had to be in a hospital so the nurses and doctors could help her get better. He missed seeing Gran and wanted to be with her. Mummy cried when he said that, and ran upstairs. Something bad had happened, but nobody would tell him. He wanted Gran and felt bewildered because she wasn't there.

'William, your Gran has died and gone to heaven,' his father said.

After that they sometimes went to a funny sort of garden with lots of big white stones. Mummy often cried and they took flowers to give Gran – but she was never there ...

Dealing with dying is tough for adults and it may feel too much to have to explain everything to a child as well. Don't ignore their questions and emotions but remember the confusion and hurt could go deep, causing problems in the future.

HELPING THEM UNDERSTAND

* *Be truthful* when a child asks about death. Although a young child does not need to know all the facts and implications, he should be kept abreast with events. Explain that sometimes people become very ill, or tired, accidents happen and everybody has to die one day. It is very sad for the people left behind but the dead person cannot feel that pain any more. The Christian belief in life after death offers a great hope which can comfort even a very small child.

Matthew, when he was almost four, became very interested in his grandparents who had died long before he was born. His mother showed him pictures, told stories and shed a tear or two as she said how much they were missed. He wondered if they could see him from where they were in heaven, and straining his eyes upwards, gave a smile and a little wave – just in case. He was thoughtful about them, concerned for his mum's sadness but felt no pain. Perhaps his young mind will be a little better prepared when he is bereaved in the future.

* *Listen and watch for signs of distress.* Give the child the opportunity to express how he feels and what he thinks. Make time for him to ask questions and find out what has happened.

* *What about the funeral?* Depending on the age of the child, his ability to cope with new experiences, his relationship with the deceased and the practicalities of the situation, you may take him or not. Discuss this with someone whose opinion and wisdom you value. Think about alternative ways the child can say his goodbyes. Show him what you have chosen for him as a memento of the person and explain that you will keep it for him until he is older.

* *Talk about the deceased person*, reminding him of the happy memories. Death need not be a total mystery and dark oblivion.

The same principles apply to all the real-life dramas that may occur in your child's early years. Parenting requires, along with hundreds of other skills, a firm grasp of psychology, philosophy and theology, because three- and four-year-olds never let up on their quest for understanding in our often very puzzling world.

Perhaps the most difficult situation parents may have to handle is if their marriage fails and their children are caught, distressed, confused, insecure and guilt-stricken, in the middle of the tragedy. Because a child under about five sees everything in relation to her own self, the break-up of home as she knows it will be very hard. Families in this predicament need all our support and encouragement as they struggle courageously through to calmer waters beyond the separation or divorce. Staying together for the sake of the children is preferable from their point of view. Recent research shows that in many cases it is better for them to live with an unhappy marriage than to experience the so-called 'clean break' of divorce.

MAKING IT ALL REAL

Children need to try things for themselves! Faith is 'better felt than tell't' as the old saying goes. As soon as your toddler can string three words together, he can talk to God – even if the theological content is a bit unreliable. He can begin learning to communicate with a God who is there and ready to listen, so perhaps there is a regular slot somewhere in your routine when a couple of minutes could become a focus for this. Find what works best for you, have confidence, and go for it! Saying Grace at meals is a natural starting point and bedtime could always include a prayer.

By the time Don and Marie's third child was born, their older two were seven and five years old and family devotions had moved from the tea-stained sheets of their bed to the breakfast table. The baby became accustomed to hearing prayers said about all kinds of things, observed stories being read from the Bible story book, accepting it all as unremarkable and routine – and loved joining in! A little older, Harry would sit in his high chair, checking that everyone had their eyes shut and maximise his moment of glory – saying Grace! 'Nankoo God buttust (breakfast), Aaaaamen!' he'd shout enthusiastically with a flourish of his spoon – and the eating could begin! Harry's grasp of all this was minimal! Who *was* God and what was the sense in thanking him when it was Mummy who had got breakfast ready? Anyway, the whole family loved his cabaret act, and little by little, Harry's understanding grew to take in some of the implications of being part of a Christian family.

One day – he was three by now – Harry said to his dad, 'You are called God.' He had obviously heard Don address God as 'Father'. Dad was extremely chuffed at this remark although the rest of the family laughed! But in a way the boy was right. Parents are meant to be the next best thing to God, and children's experience of them will colour their understanding of what the Heavenly Father is like. What a responsibility! Nobody's perfect, but our actions and words will affect the development of our children's faith in a good God.

Many people build their ideas about God on the experience of their parents' love from the first years. Many adults are unfortunate in their early experience and carry psychological scars from an unhappy childhood. This can distort their understanding of God.

If, reading this, you are worried that you have let your children down by being less than a human embodiment of perpetual sweetness and light towards them, join the club! Do not worry! Parenting is surely the most taxing of professions known to humankind, and failure and mistakes are always redeemable, especially when we ask God's help. If you have serious concerns, turn to someone who can help you.

How can we make faith relevant to the real world of small children? They will not begin to understand abstract ideas until they are much older, and it is not easy for them to distinguish fact from fantasy. A young child exists almost completely in the 'now!' of life. If the Jesus we talk about has nothing to do with the fascinating real world of tractors, cats and dogs, favourite food and best friends, he will be irrelevant to a pre-school child. At the same time, we need to be careful not to trivialise the message and allow Christ to be regarded as someone as ordinary as anyone else.

Train your child to respond to situations with prayer; encountering a fire-engine or a lady in a wheel-chair may be something to talk to God about later on – or even at the time.

Encourage him to expect answers to prayers and remind him when things he prayed about actually happen. Teach him to be grateful, thanking God for good things, healing, happy times, people ... the list goes on ...

The kiss of death to anyone's faith must be boredom! Young children need variety and information in short bytes. If, in the middle of your fascinating explanation of how Mr and Mrs Noah got the animals aboard the ark, he changes the subject completely, forget the Noahs' predicament and follow your child down his own thought tracks.

In her book, *Preparing Children to Love God*, Anna Mow writes:

Someone asked a little girl what she learned on her first day in school. She replied, 'I learned things I didn't understand and then I learned to understand them.' Most learning about God is like that at any age. We think we know something, then later a new awareness or illumination comes and we feel that we knew nothing but the words before.

Babies, toddlers, pre-school children have so much to learn – from trying to fathom who on earth God is, to mastering the zip on their jackets. They need our unconditional love, care and protection. The task of parenting is deeply satisfying, even though it may sometimes frustrate and almost defeat us! Who knows the future destiny of this person you have nurtured and loved – and will we or he ever fully comprehend the part we have played? The hours and hours spent together as our children grow will slip away from our memories. But the seeds that were sown will spring up sooner or later as the years go by and the child grows into adolescence and finally becomes an adult. The special years of early childhood pass quickly but affect us for the rest of our lives.

This morning I walked along the river-bank in the spring sunshine. Our four-year-old and his friend raced ahead of me. They chattered and chased, sang, shouted and skipped their way along, so full of zest and enthusiasm for life. We paused to throw crusts for the geese and swans, then turned to cross the road towards nursery school. Kisses and hugs, a last wave goodbye, and I left them – so eager to start this new day in their young lives – and came quietly home.

APPENDIX – LANDMARKS
AND MILESTONES

BY FOUR WEEKS

MOVING
* When held to stand can do reflex 'walking'.
* Rather a rounded back. Head often flops to one side, only staying unsupported for a moment.
* Elbows and knees bent up. Moves limbs rather jerkily, arms more than legs.
* Keeps hands closed and automatically grasps an object placed in them.
* Turns mouth to suck if touched on the cheek.

SEEING
* Can lock on to an object in front of face (three feet away) and follow it from side to side through an arc of less than ninety degrees.
* Stares at bright surfaces like windows or white walls.

HEARING
* Listens to the sound of a bell and jumps with his whole body at a sudden sound.

COMMUNICATION
* Watches mother's face when she talks – unless upset. Opens and closes mouth and bobs head at her.

AT SIX WEEKS

MOVING   * Uncurling a little and holds head up for a little longer.
       * Lifts chin for a moment when lying on his front.
       * Hands often open, grasp reflex begins to disappear.

SEEING   * Concentrates gaze on an object and follows a person moving near him with his eyes.

COMMUNICATION
       * Can be persuaded to smile and make responsive noises – specially by Mum.

THREE MONTHS

MOVING   * Body much straighter.
       * Holds head up for longer when he is upright.
       * Pushes chin and shoulders up, resting on forearms when lying on his front.
       * Hands are loosely open but may for a moment hold a rattle placed in his hand. Looks as if he would like to grasp an object but cannot unless it is placed in his hand.

SEEING AND HEARING
       * Very alert, moves head to look at something interesting like a human face.
       * Starts to watch his own hand movements.
       * Follows a dangling object through 180 degrees side to side.
       * Turns his head towards a sound.

COMMUNICATION
       * Actively enjoys bath and caring routines.
       * Squeals with pleasure and 'talks' back when spoken to.

FOUR MONTHS

MOVING
* Limbs stretched out fully.
* Only the base of back now curved.
* Head strong enough to stay up unless suddenly swayed.
* Brings hands together in play and watches them. Reaches out for objects – but usually misses. Shakes a rattle put in his hand but cannot pick it up if it drops.

SEEING
* Immediately focuses on something dangling in front of him.

COMMUNICATION
* Excited to see his food or toys, breathing fast and waving all his limbs.
* Likes to be propped up to sit.
* Laughs aloud.

FIVE MONTHS

MOVING
* Back is now straight.
* Head no longer wobbles.
* Bears much of his weight when held in a standing position.
* On front takes weight with his hands and lifts chest.
* Rolls from his front on to his back.
* Sits supported in high chair.

SEEING AND PLAYING
* Hands easily grasp objects which are often put to the mouth.
* No longer follows hand movements with eyes.
* When he drops something, looks to find it.
* Crumples paper, plays with his toes and splashes in the bath. Drops one cube when offered another.
* Holds his own bottle.

* Can drink from a cup held to his lips.

COMMUNICATION

* Complains if a toy is taken from him.
* May be excited at the sound of footsteps.
* Smiles and 'talks' to his mirror image.
* Stretches out arms to be picked up.
* May be coy with strangers.
* Shows likes and dislikes.
* Imitates cough or sticking tongue out.
* Makes sounds like 'Ah-Goo'.

SIX MONTHS

MOVING * On his back, raises head to look at feet and grasp one of them (later both).
* On his front bears weight with one hand.
* When his hands are grasped, pulls to sit.
* Sits supported by his hands.
* Begins to roll from his back on to front.
* Bounces with pleasure when held standing.

SEEING AND PLAYING

* Feeds himself with a biscuit.
* Favours preferred hand.
* Likes playing with paper.
* Bangs a toy on table and transfers it from one hand to the other.
* If holding one cube hangs on to it when offered another.
* Fascinated at everything he sees, especially adult moving about the room.

HEARING

* Deliberately shakes rattle to make the sound sometimes, looking at it at the same time.

COMMUNICATION AND SOCIAL SKILLS

* Saying single and double syllables – 'ba, da, a-a, er-leh', etc. Laughs and chuckles aloud in play. Screams in annoyance.

* Responds to his name.
* Tries attracting attention by making noise.
* Chews but keeps lips closed if he doesn't want to eat.
* Imitates simple actions.
* Pats his reflection in the mirror.
* Becomes reserved with strangers especially in mother's absence.

NINE MONTHS

MOVING
* Crawls, pulling forward with hands.
* Can sit up by himself and stay sitting steadily for ten to fifteen minutes.
* Pulls himself up to stand, holding on to furniture but cannot lower himself again without a bump.

SEEING AND PLAYING
* Uses index finger to point or poke, index finger and thumb to pick things up.
* Can begin to let things go purposely.
* Looks for and may find a hidden object.

COMMUNICATION AND SOCIAL SKILLS
* Babbles 'dad-dad, mum-mum, agaga' mainly for own amusement but also to try to communicate.
* Repeats something when it is laughed at.
* Will grasp at spoon during feeding.
* Holds, bites and chews a biscuit.
* Responds to words like 'Where is Daddy?'
* Attracts someone's attention by pulling their clothes.
* Waves 'bye-bye'. Plays 'pat-a-cake'.

ONE YEAR

MOVING
* Crawls, shuffles or walks on hands and feet like a bear. Walks forward and sideways with one hand held.
* Can pull himself up to stand and let himself down again. 'Cruises' round a room by holding on to furniture.
* May stand alone for a few moments.
* At about fourteen months may crawl upstairs.

SEEING AND PLAYING
* No longer puts everything to his mouth.
* Picks up small objects with a pincer hold.
* Plays with toys with concentration.
* Drops things to see them fall.
* Looks in the correct place for toys that have gone out of sight.
* Points at things he wants or which interest him. Likes pictures.

COMMUNICATION AND SOCIAL SKILLS
* Knows and responds to own name well. Understands several other names and instructions.
* Imitates adults' noises, actions and sometimes words.
* Speaks two or three words with meaning.

FIFTEEN MONTHS

MOVING
* Walks alone, feet wide apart, arms out for balance, with uneven steps and with little control over steering or braking.
* Kneels unaided.
* Can get upstairs and maybe down backwards.
* Generally very mobile and needs constant watching.

SEEING AND PLAYING

* Picks up small objects in either hand with a precise pincer grip. Builds a tower with two bricks when shown.
* Can scribble lines to and fro.
* Looks at pictures in book with interest.
* Asks for objects by pointing to them.
* Helps to dress, likes removing shoes.

COMMUNICATION AND SOCIAL SKILLS

* Speaks two to six recognisable words and understands many more.
* Can point to familiar people and things.
* Now feeds himself fairly efficiently.
* Beginning to say if he is wet or dirty.
* Very interested in toys and everyday objects, exploring them thoroughly. Very curious about what is going on around him.
* Can be up and down in his emotions and dependent on adult's reassuring presence.

EIGHTEEN MONTHS

MOVING * Walking well. Beginning to jump and run. Walks up and down stairs holding rail, without help.
* Pushes and pulls large floor toys.
* To sit, backs into small chair or slides in sideways but climbs up forwards into large chair then turns round. Squats down and stands up again unaided.

SEEING AND PLAYING

* Can take off gloves, socks and unzip.
* Manages spoon and cup well.
* Throws a ball without falling over.
* Turns pages in a book a few at a time.
* Builds a tower of three bricks when shown.

> * Scribbles lines and dots, usually with preferred hand.

COMMUNICATION AND SOCIAL SKILLS

> * 'Talks' a lot with great expression, especially while playing, using words, sounds and 'tunes'.
> * Uses six to twenty recognisable words and understands many more.
> * May be getting quite good at using potty (varies greatly from one child to another).
> * Copies parent in domestic jobs enjoying sweeping, dusting, washing, etc.
> * Remembers where things belong (like where the biscuit tin is kept).
> * Tries to join in nursery rhymes and may echo the last word of an adult's sentence.
> * Plays happily alone but prefers to be within reach of others.
> * Emotionally dependent on known adults.
> * Obeys simple instructions like 'Come here'.

TWO YEARS

MOVING
> * Runs safely. Climbs up to look out of window and gets back down.
> * Walks up and sometimes down stairs, two feet to each step.
> * Kicks a ball without falling over.
> * Squats down quite steadily and stands back up without using hands.
> * Pushes and pulls large wheeled toys forwards, later can walk backwards pulling toy by the handle.
> * Sits on tricycle and pushes it along with feet but cannot use the pedals.

SEEING AND PLAYING
> * Turns door knob, unscrews lids, washes and dries hands. Puts on shoes, socks, pants.

* Picks up pins and puts them down again skillfully. Unwraps a small sweet.
* Makes a tower of six or seven bricks. Turns pages singly.
* Scribbles with circular movements, imitates a vertical line and perhaps a 'V' shape.
* Recognises familiar people in photographs.

COMMUNICATION AND SOCIAL SKILLS

* May talk non-stop! – about fifty recognisable words but much still incomprehensible.
* Refers to himself by name. Puts two or more words together 'Mummy go', 'Susy want juice', etc.
* Begins to show interest in conversations around him. Constantly asking names of things. Will point correctly and repeat the words for parts of body and clothing.
* Names familiar objects and carries out simple instructions: 'Tell Daddy that tea is ready.'
* Joins in nursery rhymes and songs.
* Usually dry through the day now. Says when he needs the potty/toilet.
* Very curious about everything around him.
* Becoming very mobile but not yet able to understand or recognise common dangers.
* Constantly demands mother's attention, following her everywhere, copying her.
* Clingy if tired, fearful or unsure.
* Plays alongside other children happily but not with them. Does not easily share things.
* Wants instant gratification of his needs and desires, may throw tantrums if frustrated but can usually be distracted.

THREE YEARS

MOVING * Now very agile and able to manage stairs, simple climbing apparatus. Manoeuvres toys and himself well.

* Rides tricycle with pedals, steering round wide corners. Stands and walks on tiptoe, stands a few seconds on one foot.

* Can throw and catch a little and kicks a ball hard.

SEEING AND PLAYING

* Picks up pins with one eye covered.

* Builds tower of nine bricks and a bridge using three bricks. Threads large beads on to a lace.

* Copies an X and a circle with pencil held between first two fingers and thumb.

* Draws man with a head and a few other features or parts.

* Cuts with scissors. Enjoys painting with easel using big brush and covering the whole paper with colour. May know names of a few colours.

COMMUNICATION AND SOCIAL SKILLS

* Always asking 'What?', 'Who?', 'Where?'

* Large vocabulary using personal pronouns (he, my, us), plurals and most prepositions (up, after, out) but grammar and pronunciation often incorrect.

* Gives full name, sex and sometimes age when asked.

* Counts by rote to 10 but doesn't understand quantities beyond two or three.

* Loves stories, especially favourites.

* Eats with fork and spoon.

* Can manage most dressing except for buttons and buckles.

* Becoming more amenable and co-operative.
* Likes to help with domestic activities.
* Very inventive in play, alone and with other children. Understands about sharing, affectionate towards younger siblings.
* Shows some understanding of the need to wait for things.

FOUR YEARS

MOVING * Walks or runs up and down stairs, one foot to each step. Climbs ladders and trees. Stands, walks and runs on tiptoe. Hops on one foot. Expert tricycle rider.
* Increasing skill in ball games – begins to use a bat.

SEEING AND PLAYING
* Threads small beads on lace. Builds a set of three steps from bricks.
* Uses pencil properly; copies V, H, T, O, draws recognisable house and a man with head, legs, trunk and usually hands and fingers. Names four primary colours.

COMMUNICATION AND SOCIAL SKILLS
* Speech grammatically correct and understandable. Gives a connected account of recent events.
* Questions all the time: 'Why?', 'How?', 'When?'
* Understands concepts of past, present and future.
* Listens to and tells long stories, sometimes confusing fact and fantasy.
* Recites or sings several nursery rhymes.
* Counts to twenty by rote, understands quantities and place value to five.
* Enjoys jokes and fun.

* Brushes teeth. Dresses except for laces, back buttons and buckles.
* Becoming more independent and self-willed, can be argumentative when thwarted by adults or playmates.
* Enjoys dramatic make-believe play and dressing up.
* Needs other children's company, can take turns. Shows concern for younger siblings and other children in distress.

NOTES AND BIBLIOGRAPHY

CHAPTER 1

Thomas Verny with John Kelly, *The Secret Life of the Unborn Child* (Warner, 1993).

CHAPTER 2

Statistics by LandMARC (MARC Europe, 1993).

CHAPTER 5

A.A. Milne, *Winnie-the-Pooh* (Methuen, 1926).

CHAPTER 6

Dr James Dobson, *Parenting isn't for Cowards* (Word, 1987).

CHAPTER 7

Marion Stroud, *The Gift of a Child* (Lion, 1982).

CHAPTER 8

Dorothy Edwards, *My Naughty Little Sister Storybook* (Guild Publishing, 1991).

CHAPTER 11

'Learning for Life', Dorothy Law Nolte (originally entitled 'Children learn what they live'), *Baby Love* (Hodder & Stoughton).
Christopher Green, *Babies* (Simon & Schuster, 1989).

CHAPTER 13

Beatrix Potter, *The Tale of Peter Rabbit* (Frederick Warne).

CHAPTER 16

Marion Stroud, *The Gift of a Child* (Lion, 1982).
Anna Mow, *Preparing Your Child to Love God* (Zondervan, 1983).

The following are useful for further reading:

Ronald S. Illingworth, *The Development of the Infant and Young Child* (Churchill Livingstone, 1987).
Miriam Stoppard, *The Baby Care Book* (Dorling Kindersley, 1984).
Mary D. Sheridan, *From Birth to Five Years* (Routledge, 1993).
Susan Alexander Yates, *And Then I Had Kids* (Wolgemuth & Hyatt, 1988).
Peter Little and Derek Ralston, *The Baby Book for Dads* (New English Library, 1980).
Jean Marzollo, *Supertot, A Parent's Guide to Toddlers* (Unwin, 1984).